Pioneers of Adventure

The stories of 30 trailblazers from the mountains, the oceans, polar regions, cycling, trekking, skiing and caving

By

Roger Bunyan

Copyright © 2025 Roger Bunyan

ISBN: 978-1-918038-29-3

All rights reserved, including the right to reproduce this book, or portions thereof in any form. No part of this text may be reproduced, transmitted, downloaded, decompiled, reverse engineered, or stored, in any form or introduced into any information storage and retrieval system, in any form or by any means, whether electronic or mechanical without the express written permission of the author.

Introduction

Pioneers of Adventure is a celebration of thirty adventurers who achieved a range of breathtaking feats spanning some two hundred years. This book tells the stories of men and women who took their adventurous passions to a higher level than was the norm for the time. Unfortunately, the majority of them have been somewhat forgotten, so this is an opportunity to retell their tales.

Included are the stories of pioneering mountaineers, men and women who summited unclimbed peaks for the very first time. Such individuals were both skilled and extraordinarily daring as they made their ascents using the rudimentary equipment of the day.

Amongst these mountaineering tales includes the controversy surrounding the first ascent of Mont Blanc in the European Alps. There are stories from the Arctic, in particular of the longest journey ever made by sled across lands of the Inuit, and there is a profile of an Irish adventurer who displayed extraordinary strength and fortitude during three expeditions in the Antarctic.

Then there are the two cyclists who took their bicycles around the world during the late 1800s. There are accounts of long-distance walkers and other travellers who wished to explore our planet. There are stories of a bushwalker, an acclaimed explorer of caves, a legendary cross country skier, a record-breaking cyclist, somebody who pushed the boundaries of camping, a collapsible kayaking adventurer, the first pair to row across the Atlantic Ocean, the first to sail solo around the world – and a man who walked backwards across two continents.

Many of these characters were original thinkers, having only a vague idea of where they might be heading and the challenges that lay before them. Each of these innovative individuals from the mid-1700s to the mid-1900s had an extraordinary amount of tenacity, resilience and sheer bravery. They all possessed a unique 'derring-do' gene within their character!

Pioneers of Adventure is a follow-up book to *Against All Odds*, another book I completed about adventurers from bygone times. As before, the chapters are based on articles written for the magazine, *Wired For Adventure*. For a number of years I have been fortunate to write about historical adventurers and trailblazers in the outdoor world. The process of learning about these extraordinary people has been a joy, and I must thank *Wired For Adventure* for allowing me to use these articles for this new book.

I strongly believe that these stories should be remembered. Sadly, there is a danger these phenomenal characters' endeavours might be forgotten with time. Including them in this book will, hopefully, go some small way towards keeping their memories and accomplishments alive.

But there is another reason to tell the stories of such individuals: they might provide inspiration for future ventures. Reading these accounts could be the catalyst for a new adventure. Such endeavours may take the form of an outdoor pursuit or some other individual challenge; before you realize it you, the reader, could be planning and completing your very own journeys of derring-do. That would be such a fitting legacy for these adventurers of old, would it not?

Contents

1
Michel - Gabriel Paccard and Jacques Balmat
The story of the controversial first ascent of Mont Blanc, the highest mountain in the European Alps in 1757.

2
Benjamin Leigh Smith
A British adventurer during the 1800s who survived a winter in the Arctic with his crew and survived.

3
Ludwig Purtscheller
An Austrian who climbed extensively throughout the Alps in the 1800s and held the key to the first ascent of Kilimanjaro.

4
Snowshoe Thompson
A Norwegian-American who was famous for delivering mail to remote areas of the Sierra Nevada Mountains on skis.

5
Duke of the Abruzzi
A member of the Savoy Royal Family who was a mountaineer, Arctic explorer and an African agriculturist during the late 1800s to early 1900s.

6
Thomas Hiram Holding
The 'father' of modern day camping who designed a range of camping equipment. He wrote a number of books, inspiring many in Britain to take up camping.

7
William Sachtelban and Thomas Allen
These American adventurers were famed for their daring bicycle journey around the world between 1890 and 1893.

8
George Harbo and Frank Samuelsen
These two Norwegian migrants to the USA were the first people to row across the North Atlantic from New York to the Scilly Isles of Britain.

9
Tom Crean
An Irish Antarctic adventurer who, with extraordinary strength and fortitude, took part in three expeditions during the early 1900s.

10
Truda Benham
Truda was one of Britain's most travelled adventurers, climbing hundreds of mountains and walking thousands of kilometres across the world during the early 1900s.

11
Joshua Slocum
This seafaring Canadian-American was the first person to sail single-handedly around the world between 1895 and 1898.

12
Elizabeth Le Blond
Elizabeth Le Blond completed numerous mountaineering ascents in the Alps and the Norwegian Arctic. She was also a pioneer of mountain photography and movie-making.

13
Norman Collie
Norman Collie was a mountaineer who pioneered new climbs in Scotland and explored the mountains in the Alps, Canada, Norway and Himalaya.

14
Knud Rasmussen
Knud Rasmussen was a Greenlandic Dane who travelled extensively throughout the Arctic. He made comprehensive studies of Inuit language, traditions and customs.

15
Miriam O'Brien Underhill
Miriam O'Brien Underhill was an American who advanced the idea of climbing without guides and women-only mountaineering groups.

16
Isobel Wylie Hutchinson
Isobel Wylie Hutchinson was an Arctic traveller and botanist who travelled widely in the far north.

17
Alexandra David-Néel
Alexandra David-Néel was a Buddhist adventurer who journeyed through China, India and Tibet during the last century.

18
Alain Gerbault
Alain Gerbault sailed around the world single-handedly and was an international tennis player who settled in the Pacific Islands.

19
Norbert Casteret
Norbert Casteret was a French explorer who discovered new cave systems. With extraordinary skill he visited approximately 2000 caves during the last century.

20
Plennie Wingo
Plennie Wingo holds the world record for walking in reverse. This American man walked backwards across North America and Europe.

21
Oskar Speck
Oskar Speck travelled in a collapsible kayak from Germany to Australia.

22
Freddy Spencer Chapman
Freddy Spencer Chapman was an Arctic explorer and mountaineer who had a lifelong passion for the natural world.

23
Ang Tharkay
Ang Tharkay is considered to be one of the most outstanding Sherpa mountaineers of the last century.

24
Walter Greaves
Walter Greaves was a one-armed cyclist who broke the World Year Cycle Endurance Mileage Record in 1936.

25
Loulou Boulaz
Loulou Boulaz was one of the most successful female mountaineers and a gifted international alpine skier of the 1900s.

26
Dot Butler
Dot Butler was an Australian bushwalker, mountaineer and conservationist who was renowned for journeying barefoot.

27
Junko Tabei

Junko Tabei, a Japanese mountaineer, was the first woman to climb Mount Everest and to climb the Seven Summits, the highest point of each continent.

Chapter 1

Michel-Gabriel Paccard *Jacques Balmat*

Michel-Gabriel Paccard and Jacques Balmat

They stepped onto the summit of Mont Blanc at around 6:30 pm, at an altitude of 4877 metres.

Michel-Paccard and Jacques Balmat were the first people to climb Mont Blanc, the highest mountain in the Alps. The event took place in 1786 and has been hailed as the beginning of modern-day mountaineering.

Their early lives

Michel-Gabriel was born in 1757, the youngest of three sons, part of an established Chamonix family whose father was a local solicitor. As a child growing up in the French Alps, the ever-present image of Mont Blanc loomed over him.

As he grew older, Michel-Gabriel developed an interest in the scientific world, especially botany and other natural sciences. When he was eighteen years old he moved to Turin, the capital of Savoy, to study medicine. After that, he continued his medical studies in Paris before returning to Chamonix as a practicing doctor at the age of twenty-six.

Michel-Gabriel was a modest character with an energetic personality and he developed an ambition to climb Mont Blanc. By 1775, he had started making tentative excursions onto the mountain with a few others who were keen to climb to greater heights. He crossed some of the glaciers and was successful in getting to the lower slopes of the Aiguille du Goûter and to the Tête Rousse, both at around 3000 metres on the massif. Michel-Gabriel primarily viewed the mountain in scientific terms and longed to be the first person to take instrument readings from Mont Blanc's summit.

Jacques Balmat was from a humbler background. He was born in 1762 in the village of Pèlerins near Chamonix on a traditional alpine farm. Rather than live a life entirely from the land, Jacques wanted a more lucrative future. As a young man he became a crystal and chamois hunter, hoping this would lead to greater riches. As a result, he became an expert in scrambling around the rocky landscape and crossing glaciers in search of both crystals and chamois. He also assisted in some of the earlier journeys onto the mountain when visitors arrived.

One traveller to the region was Horace Bénédict du Saussure, a geologist, meteorologist, physicist and alpine explorer from Geneva. During his many journeys across the Alps, Horace had visited Chamonix and become obsessed with Mont Blanc. He was keen for the mountain to be climbed and offered a reward to the first person who successfully scaled the peak, although the exact amount of this prize is unknown. Indeed, Horace had dreams of scaling the massive mountain himself one day.

The thought of gaining a financial reward for climbing Mont Blanc was of immediate interest to Jacques, who was always keen to make money.

The first ascent of Mont Blanc

For centuries mountains had been regarded as the domain of evil spirits and were seen as places to avoid. Apart from hunters, the only other people to venture into the mountains were scientists studying botany and geographical features such as glaciers. Indeed, the mountains of the Mont Blanc region were so feared that they became known as the 'accursed mountains!'

Over the years attitudes gradually changed and a handful of adventurous individuals started to explore the glaciers and lower slopes. A few attempts were made to climb to the top of Mont Blanc, but on each occasion these pioneers of mountain travel were foiled by difficult conditions. Little by little, however, experience was slowly gained as people climbed ever higher upon the rock, snow and ice of this highest of alpine mountains.

In June 1786, whilst Jacques was searching for crystals, he joined a group making an attempt to reach the summit. Unfortunately, he became separated from the rest of the party and had to spend the night out in the snow high up on Mont Blanc. At the time people thought this was impossible, but he proved that a person could stay outside and survive in the snow at high altitude. After this excursion, Jacques was so badly sunburnt that he consulted Dr Michel-Gabriel Paccard in Chamonix. During his treatment, the two men discussed their experiences of various routes on the mountain.

For the previous three years, Michel-Gabriel had been viewing Mont Blanc from high up on le Brévant, a vantage point across the Chamonix valley; from there he could clearly see its northern side. Looking through a telescope, he had worked out a possible route to the top by way of forest, rocky outcrops and glaciers that would eventually lead to the snow dome upon the mountain's very summit.

Michel-Gabriel's observations involved many hours of studying the upper snow-slopes during different seasons and times of day. Jacques' information that it was possible to bivouac high up on the mountain in the snow was important, and the two men agreed to join forces in a fresh bid to become the first people to climb to the top of Mont Blanc.

They made an unlikely partnership: Michel-Gabriel, a scientist, wanted to be the first to take readings from the highest point in the Alps; Jacques wanted to claim Horace Bénédict de Saussure's reward for being the first to climb Mont Blanc. Michel-Gabriel wasn't interested in any financial reward and was happy to leave any prize money to Jacques.

After waiting three weeks for the weather to settle, they started their journey in the early afternoon of August 7, 1786. During those early days of mountain exploration, there were many unknowns to hinder upward progress: weather conditions; the state of the snow; dangerous crevasses; identifying a suitable route, as well as coping with the altitude. They had to consider all this whilst using very basic eighteenth-century equipment.

The men wore homespun jackets and trousers and carried one blanket between them. They took a little food and Michel-Gabriel's rudimentary scientific instruments; they also both carried a 2.5 metre baton, a wooden pole with an iron spike at one end. This would be particularly useful when travelling across glaciers and probing for crevasses. Additionally, Jacques carried a wood-axe for chopping ice, but they had no ropes, mountaineering ice-axes or crampons!

From Chamonix, they went up the Montagne de la Côte, a finger of forest, rock and moraine rising out of a valley between two glaciers. They spent the night under a huge granite boulder at the top at an altitude of about 2500 metres; this bivouac area is still there today and is known as the Gîte à Balmat.

They left at 4 am and started their journey across the Glacier des Bossons. The weather was settled, but many of the snow-bridges across the crevasses had melted because of the hot summer, necessitating some delicate route-finding through a maze of steep ice and gaping crevasses.

Michel-Gabriel wrote:

Four times the snow bridges, by which we tried to cross the crevasses, gave way beneath our feet, and we saw the abyss below us. But we escaped a catastrophe by throwing ourselves flat on our batons laid horizontally on the snow, and then, placing our two batons side by side, we slid along them until we were across the crevasse.

It took them eight hours to find a way through the glacial ice to the rocky outcrop of the Grands Mulets at just over 3000 metres. After crossing the glacier, Jacques was now exceedingly tired but Michel-Gabriel urged him on and carried his pack.

Struggling with the heat and the altitude, Jacques suggested they abandon the climb; he said he wished to return to Chamonix to attend to his sick baby. However, they kept going and crossed le Grand Plateau, taking it in turns to lead through the snow and to avoid falling into crevasses.

It was exhausting work because the melting snow continued to give way under their weight and they were blinded by the glare of the sun reflecting off the snow, but by five o'clock they were above the Rochers Rouges at around 4550 metres, and looking for a place to bivouac for the night. Finding nothing, they plodded on.

Still climbing upwards, they reached the steepest and most exposed section of the ascent at an approximate forty-degree angle. The snow had suddenly become very hard and they had to make footholds into the surface with their batons. To add to their difficulties, an extremely cold north-west wind had started to blow, which carried Michel-Gabriel's hat over into Courmayeur.

He later wrote:

We had to stop every hundred steps...to regain breath and strength...the higher we got...every fourteen paces.

Michel-Gabriel and Jacques continued upwards until they reached the top; it was a remarkable pioneering feat using only their batons and carrying cumbersome scientific equipment. They stepped onto the summit of Mont Blanc at around 6:30pm, at an altitude of 4806 metres, the first men to climb to the highest point in the Alps!

As planned, Michel-Gabriel tried to carry out some scientific observations by taking both thermometer and barometer readings, but he found the process almost impossible. He was tired, cold, hungry and feeling the effects of altitude. In addition, his hands were frostbitten and his eyes were swollen and painful from the continual glare of the sun.

Amazingly, their progress to the summit had been witnessed by a number of people down in Chamonix who had been following their journey by telescope; hoping to be seen, Jacques spent time waving towards the village.

After half an hour they started down; with barely two and a half hours of daylight left they moved as quickly as they could, running and sliding wherever possible. Fortunately, as the sun finally disappeared beneath the horizon, a bright moon appeared to light their way.

With the sun gone, the temperature dropped significantly so the snow hardened, making their descent much easier, especially when they were on snow bridges over crevasses. At about midnight, having been on the move for twenty hours, Michel-Gabriel and Jacques reached the top of the Montagne de la Côte. Exhausted, and suffering physically from their ordeal, they wrapped themselves in their one blanket and tried to rest as they shivered in their cold bivouac.

The next morning they continued down the mountainside into Chamonix, by which time Michel-Gabriel was almost completely snow-blind and being led by Jacques.

After the climb

Michel-Gabriel met with local friends and some German visitors to Chamonix who had been following the expedition through telescopes. A very contented man, he said,

> 'We have been where no living being has ever been before, not even the eagle and the chamois.'

Word soon spread of this historical feat. As soon as he could, Jacques travelled to Geneva to inform Horace Bénédict de Saussure that Mont Blanc had finally been climbed and the event had been witnessed by a number of onlookers. He was presented with his reward, a payment that had been waiting for someone to earn for twenty-six years!

Marc Bourrit, who lived in Geneva, listened to Jacques' account of their ascent of Mont Blanc. A well-known artist and writer of alpine travel books, he had made earlier attempts to climb Mont Blanc but had disagreed with Michel-Gabriel Paccard during one of these trips. Hearing the news of the successful climb, Marc became extremely jealous of his old adversary's success. He believed that he should have had the glory of being first to the summit, not the Chamonix doctor!

As he listened to the story, he intimated that such a daring ascent must surely have been entirely due to the leadership of Jacques Balmat! Before long, Marc had manipulated and altered the entire tale, and unfortunately Jacques made no effort to correct his changes.

In truth, Jacques preferred this new version of the ascent that made him out to be quite the hero. The acclaim for climbing Mont Blanc had gone to his head, making him somewhat boastful and conceited. In the altered story, Michel-Gabriel was pictured as the weaker of the pair, requiring a great deal of help to get to the top, while Jacques had to continually stop to drag him upwards; supposedly, at one point, Michel-Gabriel had been so tired he was crawling on all fours! The new version made the doctor out to be an extremely weak, helpless, almost buffoon-like character!

Michel-Gabriel was very upset when he learned about the new interpretation of their ascent; in fact, he insisted that Jacques sign an affidavit denying Marc Bourrit's false version. However, it was futile because Marc was such an established authority on the Alps that most people believed him. The new account was published first in newspapers and then made into a book, *The First Ascent Of Mont Blanc; A True Story by Jacques Balmat*. This extract from the publication illustrates some of the falsifications:

I lifted my head, and, lo! And behold!...I had conquered Mont Blanc!...The first moment of exultation over, I thought of my poor Doctor...I descended as quickly as possible, calling out his name...I found him with his head between his knees...I took him by the shoulder...I told him that I had reached the summit of Mont Blanc...in reply he asked where he could go to bed and to sleep...I took him by the shoulders and made him walk...At six o'clock I was once more on the summit of Mont Blanc, and with my worthy Doctor too.

Jacques Balmat acquired both fame and fortune from his ascent of Mont Blanc. In addition to de Saussure's prize money, he was awarded a gratuity by King Victor Amadeus III, the King of Sardinia who ruled the Chamonix region as part of Savoy. The king gave him the honorary title of Balmat du Mont Blanc and he received money collected by the German dignitary, Baron von Gersdorf, who had witnessed the ascent. With such wealth, Jacques eventually built a new chalet in Chamonix for his family. His life was changed yet further when he was employed as an official Mont Blanc guide.

In 1787, Horace Bénédict de Saussure succeeded in making his own ascent of Mont Blanc, a year after Michel-Gabriel and Jacques. His journey to the summit was a huge affair that included 20 guides and servants, the chief guide being Jacques Balmat. Horace took a tent, folding bed, mattress, sheets, blankets, eight coats, six shirts, boots, three pairs of shoes and a pair of slippers!

He successfully climbed to the top of the mountain, where he spent a total of four-and-a-half hours conducting scientific experiments. An account of his journey was published in a book that became a huge success. Due to Horace's climb and the subsequent publicity, many more visitors started to visit the Chamonix region.

Later life

Michel-Gabriel continued working as a physician in Chamonix and made several more journeys into the mountains. He wrote his own account of the first ascent but it was never printed having been forestalled by Marc Bourrit's brother in-law, who was publishing the book in Geneva.

Despite the disagreements about the Mont Blanc climb, in 1796 Michel-Gabriel married Jacques' sister, Marie, ten years after the first ascent. Later in life he became the Justice of Peace for Chamonix. He died in 1827, sadly never having been recognised as playing an equal role in achieving Mont Blanc's first-ever ascent.

As for Jacques, he continued guiding people onto Mont Blanc and in total he made eight more ascents. He also became a member of the council for the local commune. He failed in his attempt to introduce Merino sheep into the Chamonix valley and eventually gave up guiding in favour of searching for gold in the nearby Sixt valley. Unfortunately he died in 1834 after falling from a cliff while he was mining.

In 1887, in celebration of 100 years since the first ascent of Mont Blanc, a bronze monument was erected in Chamonix; however, it only displayed Jacques Balmat pointing up to the summit of Mont Blanc with Horace Bénédict de Saussure looking upwards. Michel-Gabriel was absent from the monument, having been all-but written out of the story.

Throughout the 1800s and into the next century, Jacques continued to be regarded as the hero and Michel-Gabriel the weaker of the two climbers, but towards the end of the 1800s, British, Swiss and American individuals started investigating the details of that first ascent of Mont Blanc and gradually pieced together a different narrative.

It became clear that Michel-Gabriel and Jacques had worked together as equals during their quest to reach the top of Mont Blanc, and this is now accepted as the true version even though Michel-Gabriel's written account of the journey has never been found.

To celebrate the bicentenary of the climb, another bronze statue was erected in Chamonix in 1986. To help correct the historical injustice, this was of Michel-Gabriel and was situated 150 meters away from the Balmat/du Saussure statue in a gesture to correct the false version of that first ascent more than a century after Michel-Gabriel's death in 1827.

Although acrimony was part of the story, it shouldn't lessen the importance of such a milestone in mountaineering history. The climb was a daring ascent into unexplored heights. The two pioneering climbers used only a long pole with an iron tip to make their way on an untravelled route exposed to cold, altitude, sun-glare and dangerous slopes. A phenomenal amount of effort and skill must have been required to make their way around and over the many crevasses.

The days of visiting such high places only to hunt for crystals and chamois, or for scientific study, were on the wane. The first ascent of Mont Blanc helped trigger a more positive interest in mountains and heralded the beginning of modern-day mountaineering.

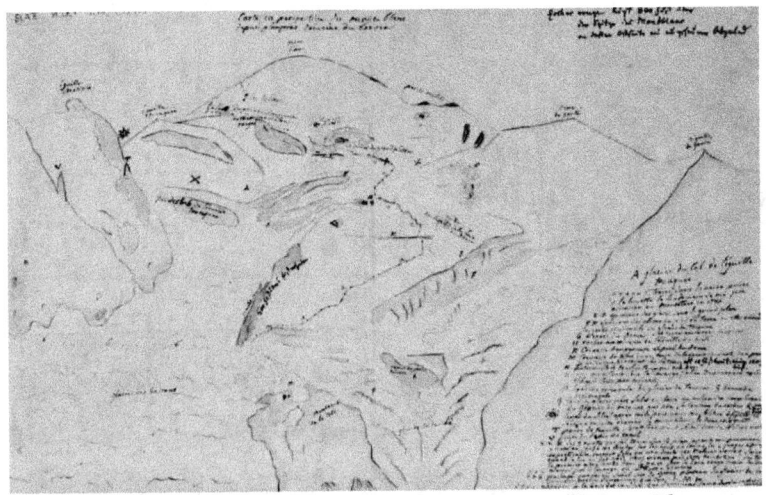

Diagram of their route on the first ascent of Mont Blanc (Credit: Summit Post)

Mont Blanc as seen from Le Brévant (Credit: Chamonix Tourist Office)

*Gîte a Balmat where they bivouaced on the way to the summit
(Credit: Camptocamp)*

Mont Blanc north facing side

Statue of Dr Michel-Gabriel Facing Mont Blanc

Statue of Jacques Balmat pointing to the summit of Mont Blanc with Horace Benedict du Saussure looking

Chapter 2

Benjamin Leigh Smith

Benjamin Leigh Smith - Portrait by Stephen Pearce

All 25 members of the Eira had survived the sinking of their ship, as well as an Arctic winter and a journey in open boats across iceberg peppered waters!

Benjamin Leigh Smith was a British Arctic explorer and sea captain who discovered new areas of Arctic Svalbard and Franz Josef Land between 1871 and 1882. After being stranded on an Arctic island for almost a year during one of his journeys, he and his crew managed to escape to safety without any loss of life.

Earlier life

Benjamin Leigh Smith was born in 1828 into a wealthy but somewhat unconventional and radical thinking family for the Victorian era. He was born out of wedlock, along with four other siblings, which was deemed scandalous for the times.

His mother was a milliner called Anne Longden; his Whig politician father, also called Benjamin Smith, worked tirelessly for the abolition of the slave trade. Their son, Benjamin, eventually went to Cambridge University to train to become a barrister with the intention of fighting for women's equality.

During his time at university, Benjamin excelled in outdoor activities: he became a good shot and was a very competent yachtsman. However, rather than take up a career in law as expected, he decided to complete a ship-master's certificate that would prove his ability to sail a vessel at sea. He had sufficient personal wealth as a landowner to live comfortably without ever having to work – and he decided to follow his dream of exploring the little-known frozen world of the Arctic.

Expeditions to Svalbard

In 1871 Benjamin realised his ambition by taking a sailing ship named *Sampson* to the Arctic. The expedition made its way to the Svalbard archipelago situated midway between Norway and the North Pole. Although other prominent explorers from a number of European nations had already visited these waters, due to the physical challenges they presented there was still much more to discover. Benjamin set about exploring these remote islands.

Manoeuvring any ship using only sails wasn't always straightforward because of the ever-changing weather and sea-ice. During the nineteenth century, the Arctic ice pack was thicker and came much further south during the summer months than is the case today.

Benjamin quickly developed a simple philosophy when it came to exploration, which was to be guided entirely by circumstances. If the ice prevented him travelling in one direction, he could always try somewhere else that offered more favourable conditions.

During this five-month long expedition he achieved a great deal, discovering and surveying a total of 22 previously unknown islands; furthermore, he logged an additional 33 coastal and land locations.

Benjamin undertook oceanographic studies by taking temperature readings at various depths to help determine the nature of ocean currents in the region. This was pioneering research and produced a large quantity of data. He catalogued both land and sea fauna and flora, with the results destined for the British Museum and the Royal Botanical Gardens.

As the season came to a close, the increase in sea-ice started to hamper further progress. Benjamin sailed as far as he could go north of the island of Rossoya; he was already considering a possible future journey to the North Pole. However, on reaching a wall of pack-ice at 81 degrees 25 minutes north, he had to turn back.

The following year Benjamin journeyed north once again in *Sampson* to continue his exploration and research. On his way to Svalbard, he explored volcanic Jan Mayen Island equidistant between Greenland, Iceland and Norway. Returning to Svalbard, the expedition continued its scientific enquiries, and attempts were made to explore a variety of locations, but during the 1872 summer season there was far more ice to contend with. On several occasions their vessel was trapped in ice, which damaged the hull. As a result, the ship had to be beached on an uncharted island in order to carry out repairs.

The following season, on his third trip to Svalbard, Benjamin took two vessels: a steamship named *Diana,* and *Sampson* as a support ship. During their journey he learned of the plight of the Swedish explorer Adolf Erik Nordenskiöld; he had been overwintering in the islands ready for a push to the North Pole but two of his supply ships had become marooned in ice! Sixty-seven people from three different ships had to survive the long winter on rations from just one ship. Food was running out and some of them were suffering from scurvy.

Benjamin arrived just in time and was able to leave them sufficient supplies to see them through the weeks until the Swedes' vessels were no longer ice bound. For giving this much-needed assistance, the King of Sweden awarded Benjamin the Polar Star medal in 1873. It was assumed that the British government might also honour him but, as he remained a somewhat controversial and unconventional figure with an illegitimate background, such recognition wasn't forthcoming. This suited Benjamin because he always shunned the limelight. Even the award given by the King of Sweden had to be sent to him by post because he made himself unavailable for the ceremony. Like other explorers, Benjamin enjoyed the adventure – but unlike most others he did not enjoy the glory!

The first expedition to Franz Josef Land

By 1880, Benjamin was ready to travel northward for his fourth Arctic adventure. For this trip he had a purpose-built steamship, *Eira,* specially designed and built for Arctic travel which was capable of cutting through sea-ice with a one-metre thick hull and bows almost 2.5 metres thick.

Benjamin returned to Svalbard, but again the pack ice prevented *Eira* from travelling any further north so he decided to sail eastwards to the relatively unknown Franz Josef Land. Steaming along the southern limit of the pack ice, *Eira* was more adept at steering around icebergs and eventually made her way to the islands.

It was time for more oceanographic research as well as general exploration; during the following weeks the ship visited more than 200 kilometres of hitherto previously unknown territory including new islands, coastal features and waterways.

Whenever they discovered new islands, a pattern emerged. First a party landed, then they climbed to the top of the island wherever possible and gave it a name. In total, they discovered eleven new islands and logged dozens of new locations.

Benjamin took great delight in naming new geographical features after colleagues, prominent individuals and family members. Amongst these were Cape Flora named after a cousin, Bell Island after his sister, and Nightingale Sound after Florence Nightingale, his famous nursing cousin.

As ice conditions deteriorated, the summer's explorations were over, but after ten years of journeying Benjamin Leigh Smith had become Britain's leading Arctic traveller.

Shipwreck and survival

The following summer Benjamin returned to Franz Joseph Land but found the sea around the islands filled with a great deal of ice; by the 21st of August, *Eira* was completely ice bound just a few kilometres from Cape Flora on Northbrook Island.

The pressure became too great and *Eira* was trapped between giant icebergs. Tragedy: she began to flounder, take in water and sink! All hands set to, in order to salvage as much as possible – the ship was carrying enough food supplies to last the 25-strong crew for two years. Fortunately, they were able to offload most of these together with numerous other items.

After a few hours of frantic work, the crew watched their ship finally sink. They were now stranded and needed to work out how to survive through the winter on an Arctic island no human had ever lived on before.

After a cold night on the ice, they dragged their supplies and four small boats onto the shore five kilometres away. Benjamin Leigh Smith, with his calm demeanor and natural ability as leader, came into his own and convinced his crew that by being disciplined and using their survival skills they would get through the ordeal.

Using boulders and salvaged bits of ship, they constructed a 12 metres long, 3.5 metres wide and 1.9 metres high hut. They used *Eira*'s sails for the roof and filled in any gaps in the stone walls with turf. They built the rough structure in sixteen days and named it Flora Cottage. All the crew had an individual place to sleep, and there was a kitchen for cooking and storing food supplies. They had coal to cook with and walrus blubber to burn for heating.

Benjamin organised a routine to get them through the months of total darkness and the intense cold of an Arctic winter. Before the days became completely dark, groups went out to hunt polar bears, walrus and birds to supplement their food supplies. By using their island bounty and *Eira*'s stores, the crew were well fed and had enough to drink within a relatively warm hut. They spent much of the winter chatting, playing cards, reading and yarn telling. Every Saturday evening the men were given a double ration of grog and the musical instruments from *Eira* were brought out; a grand sing-song would ensue with the evening always ending in an enthusiastic rendition of 'Rule Britannia'!

On the 4th of January, they recorded their lowest temperature: - 42 degrees Celsius; it was possibly even colder but that was the lowest gradient on the thermometer! By the end of January, a little light had started to appear in the sky, allowing groups to go out hunting for more food. There had been a few occasions during the long winter when polar bears had attempted to attack the stranded crew.

By March it was time to prepare *Eira*'s small boats for their escape. They repaired any damage, made them watertight and constructed masts. *Eira*'s sails couldn't be used since they had been required for Flora Cottage, so tablecloths, shirts and anything else that would hold wind were used in their place.

They waited for enough sea-ice to melt and eventually the boats, loaded with supplies, were dragged into open water on the 21st of June. Benjamin intended to make for Matochkin Strait, a location in Novoya Zemlya, 360 kilometres to the south. This was a popular fjord for whaling ships and other vessels to take shelter during periods of bad weather. Even though it was a long distance away, they believed it was their best chance of rescue.

Their journey in the four boats was initially hindered by a lack of continual open water; they often found themselves unable to sail or even row for any distance but had to manoeuvre gingerly around blocks of ice. Sometimes their progress was completely blocked, requiring them to haul boats onto the ice and wait for open water to appear. Occasionally they were marooned for days, camping out on icy platforms; at other times, they endured raging storms and strong winds.

Adding to their slow progress, some vessels began taking in too much water and needed emergency repairs. A further threat to their lives came on the ice they hauled upon overnight; in steadily warming conditions, some of these floes started to disintegrate, making sleep hazardous.

Fortunately, they eventually found themselves in open water and made better progress even though the crafts continually needed to be bailed out. They were in constant fear of capsizing. Morale was very low but they kept going. Remarkably, after three weeks they spotted a ship as they neared the Arctic island of Novoya Zemlya. It was a rescue ship, *Hope,* one of three which had been sent to locate the besieged crew. The men were ecstatic!

All 25 members of the *Eira* had survived the sinking of their ship, as well as an Arctic winter and a journey in open boats across iceberg peppered waters! Their survival and escape to safety has to be one of greatest stories in marine history.

Later life

There was celebration when the world learnt of the crew's survival story. Friends and family were relieved to learn that they were all safe, and Benjamin's leadership was particularly applauded. One of the greatest whaling captains of the day, David Gray, described Benjamin as having *'quiet, cool, thoroughbred English pluck'*.

However, just as before Benjamin played down his role in the story and avoided accolades. Even when Queen Victoria asked to look at the photographs of his Arctic adventure, he made himself unavailable and sent his brother-in-law instead. Unlike most other adventurers throughout history, this modest man had no desire to give talks or write books about his journeys; as a consequence, he has largely been forgotten and few people know about his extraordinary achievements.

In 1887 he married Charlotte Sellers and they had two sons: Benjamin in 1888, followed by Philip in 1892. This remarkable man retired from seafaring and settled down to a quieter life with his family and friends whilst looking after the affairs of his considerable estate.

He had become one of the foremost Arctic explorers of his day and achieved so much during his five expeditions. His exploration of Svalbard and Franz Joseph Land helped many others make plans for future Arctic journeys, and the huge amount of data he collected on his expeditions helped in the understanding of oceanography, climate and other facets of science. He died in 1913 aged 85.

Flora Cottage (Credit:Marie-France Le Fel)

Inside the hut (Credit: Marie-France Le Fel)

The steamship Eira (Credit: NI Public Records Office)

*On board the Eira in 1880.
Benjamin Leigh Smith, second from left*

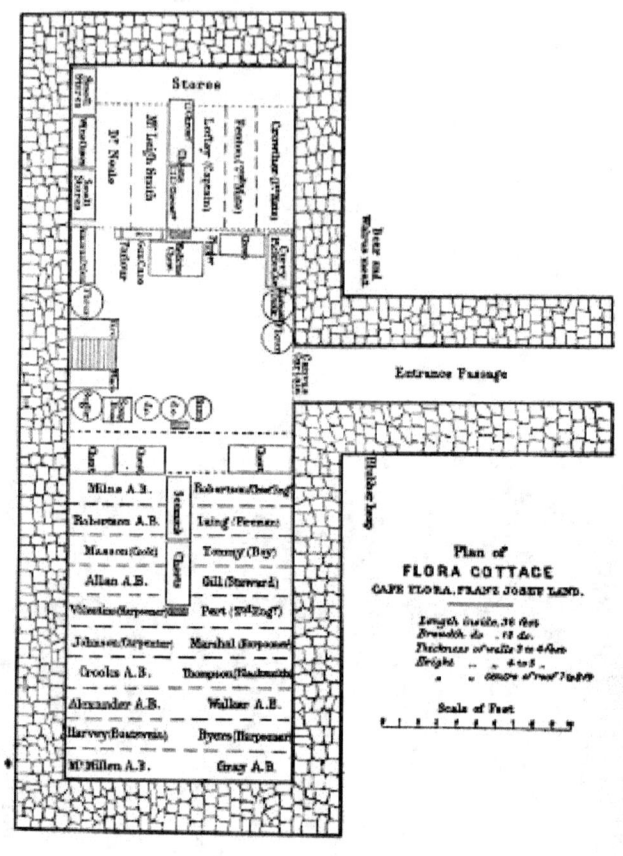

Plan of Flora Cottage (Credit-Marie-France Le Fel)

The sinking of the Eira (Credit: Marie-France Le Fel)

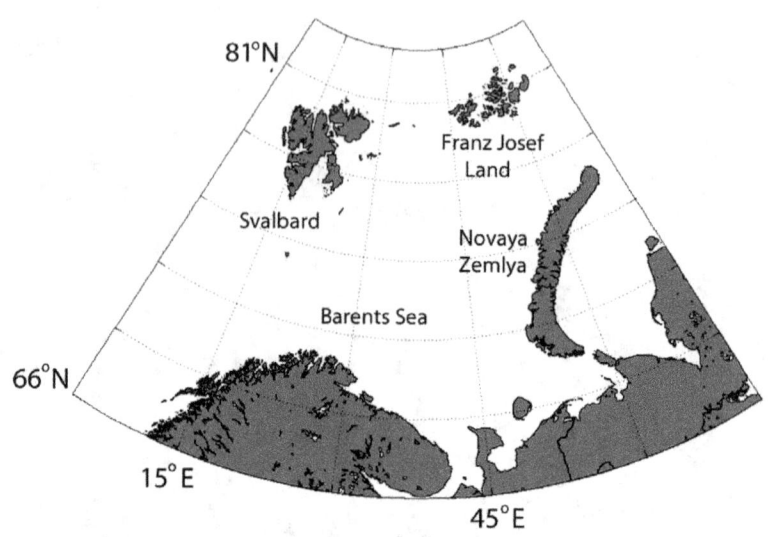

The location of the three archipelagoes surrounding the Barents Sea

Chapter 3

Ludwig Purtscheller

Ludwig Purtscheller

He became legendary in the total number of mountains he ascended.

Ludwig Purtscheller was an Austrian mountaineer during the late 1800s. He is renowned for his prolific climbing record and for ascending mountains across the Alps without a guide. Guide-less climbing was considered revolutionary at the time. He also provided the expertise for the first ascent of Kilimanjaro, Africa's highest peak.

Early life

Ludwig was born in 1849 into a family of modest means in Innsbruck, Austria. At the age of sixteen he found employment in an office of the Bleiberger Mining Company in the city of Villach, where he learnt a great deal about mineralogy and geology. Unfortunately he found working indoors tedious because, even as a young child, he had always been very energetic.

In pursuit of a more active working life, he decided to complete a physical education teaching course. After his training, he found a job teaching gymnastics in a school in the Austrian city of Klagenfurt; he then moved to Salzburg where he continued his career in education by teaching both gymnastics and writing.

A life in the mountains

It was during his early life that Ludwig started to visit the mountains to fulfil his craving for more physical activity. These initial trips instilled both a passion for the mountains and a love of climbing.

From the lower, less demanding peaks he gradually progressed to higher and more challenging climbs, steadily building up his experience and understanding of how to ascend mountains, each of which presented different challenges. Over time, his excursions saw him travelling further afield across all the Eastern Alps and then to the mountains of Styria, Salzburgerland, North Tyrol and the Bavarian Alps.

From these initial forays, it was apparent that Ludwig preferred to find his own way up peaks; this was quite radical at a time when climbing in the Alps was almost exclusively in the company of a guide. He visited new mountainous areas whenever he had the opportunity with friends and sometimes on his own, in poor weather conditions and on terrain that offered a variety of demands.

All his climbing companions enjoyed the same pioneering values as Ludwig; they included the Austrian brothers Otto and Emil Zsigmondy, who also preferred climbing guide-less. Ludwig and his friends were pushing the limits of mountaineering to a new level and had a reputation for daring and extreme climbing.

Around 1883, Ludwig started to explore the Western Alps. His list of successful ascents continued to increase; his new climbing triumphs included the first crossing of the Meije as well as challenging climbs on Monte Rosa, Bietschorn, Täschorn, Grand Jorasses and Dent Blanche. In 1884 Ludwig and two friends completed the first guide-less crossing of the Matterhorn.

Most of these climbs involved difficult routes and many had not been done before. Among these successes was Purtscheller Peak in the French Alps, which was a first ascent and was named in his honour. The rate at which Ludwig ascended mountains in the Alps was phenomenal: on some days it wasn't uncommon for him to climb several peaks in one day!

As time went by, his exploits were discussed by fellow mountaineers in the region as he had become one of the most gifted and prolific mountain climbers in the whole of Europe.

The first ascent of Kilimanjaro

Due to Ludwig's growing status, in 1889 he was invited to climb Kilimanjaro in German East Africa by a German geographer, Hans Meyer. Two years previously Meyer had failed to climb the mountain's steep and ice-clad summit, so he invited Ludwig to accompany him after he learned about his impressive feats in the Alps. Meyer was determined to be the first to climb this iconic peak but he needed the technical mountaineering know-how of an experienced alpinist. He once said,

...the highest mountain in Germany must first be climbed by a German.

At that time, Kilimanjaro was in Tanganyika, part of German East Africa. After being thwarted by the challenging climbing required for ascending this high altitude mountain, Meyer was convinced that Ludwig held the key to his eventual success.

Another reason why the previous attempt had failed was because of the lack of supplies in the upper reaches of the mountain, which had resulted in expedition members having to descend the mountainside to replenish food and other items. In Meyer's new expedition, camps were planned at different places up the mountainside that would be continually re-stocked by porters from villages at the base of Kilimanjaro. The climbers could then remain high up on the mountain and would have a greater chance of success.

Before any attempts to scale the mountain could take place, the expedition had a difficult 14-day trek from the port of Mombasa on the Indian Ocean to Taveta village on the south-eastern side of Kilimanjaro. The expedition entourage included a Somali security force, a host of local porters and the climbers themselves. From Taveta it was possible to start their ascent. Eventually a final camp was made at a point where they could begin their attempt on the summit.

During the late 1800s there was far more snow and ice on Kilimanjaro than in modern times: the glaciers were far longer, more snow fell on the mountain and at lower elevations. Eventually, Ludwig and Hans left their highest camp at 4,300 metres, made their way steadily upwards and eventually arrived at the Ratzel Glacier.

Ludwig, the alpinist, came into his own as he cut steps with his ice-axe up the icy surface. Slowly and steadily they ascended the snow and ice onto the rim of Kilimanjaro's crater and eventually arrived at a point 150 metres from the top of the colossal mountain, but they were both struggling in the thin air and deep snow so they returned to their camp to gather their strength.

Three days later, suitably rested, they followed their previous route and this time continued to the top. They had become the first people to climb to the highest point in all of Africa at an altitude of 5895m. Ludwig wrote:

...we approached the highest edge, half a hundred laborious steps in the most exalted expectation, when the earth opened before us...

He added:

This is a wonderful birthday present for me, today I am 40 years old.

They named the highest point on Kilimanjaro, Kaiser Wilhelm Peak after the German Emperor. It was an incredible occasion in mountaineering history, all thanks to Ludwig and his technical know-how.

After the ascent, they reconnoitered other summits on the nearby peaks of Mawenzi on the eastern side of Kilimanjaro. Climbing on steep rock was extremely challenging and technical, and they attempted several exploratory climbs before they eventually climbed one of the pinnacles. They named this Purtscheller Peak; it was later renamed Klute Peak.

<u>Later life</u>

In 1891 Ludwig went to the Caucasus Mountains and climbed the highest mountain in Europe, Mount Elbrus at 5642m. His party also climbed a number of other peaks in the range. During the following years he frequently climbed mountains throughout the Alps.

In 1895 he married Hedwig Helmreich von Brunnenfeld and they had a baby girl. Unfortunately Ludwig was attacked by typhus in the same year, which temporarily put a halt to any climbing.

As he explored the mountains and gained more experience of different Alpine locations, he started writing about them. He wrote a number of articles and guidebooks to assist fellow alpinists including: *High Tourist in the Eastern Alps*; *Over Rock and Firn – Mountain Walks*; *The Development of the Eastern Alps*; *Salzburg Limestone Alps* and *Stubai Alps*. He was one of the first mountaineers to write both books and articles and continued to do so into his later years.

His last climb was on the difficult Aiguille du Dru in the French Alps in 1899. On this occasion Ludwig had decided to climb with two guides. As they descended from the summit an ice axe broke, which resulted in the three roped mountaineers falling into a crevasse. Ludwig had broken his arm, but fortunately they all managed to descend the mountain and he was taken to hospital.

Sadly, after spending several months recovering, he contracted pneumonia and died. At his eulogy in 1900 a fellow climber, the American W.A.B. Coolidge described him as being *'the greatest mountaineer who had ever lived'*.

Ludwig Purtscheller, one of the first mountaineers in the Alps to climb without using guides, undoubtedly encouraged many others to climb independently. He became legendary because of the number of mountains he ascended: he climbed more than 1,700 peaks in a mountaineering career that lasted some 24 years. Remarkably, more than 40 of these were more than 4000 metres in height. Such statistics are staggering given the pioneering nature of climbing during that period – and, of course, he will be remembered for the significant part he played in the first ascent of Kilimanjaro in 1889. Ludwig opened the way for future explorations of this iconic mountain.

Alpinism in the late 1800s

Kilimanjaro in the late 1800s

Climbing in the Alps

Ludwig climbing in the Alps

Reaching the summit of Kilimanjaro

Chapter 4

Snowshoe Thompson

Snowshoe Thompson

He flew down the steep mountainside holding his long pole horizontally like a tightrope walker. On other occasions he would sway it from side to side, 'as a soaring eagle dips its wings'.

John 'Snowshoe' Thompson was a Norwegian migrant to the United States during the 1800s. He became well known for his heroic delivery of mail to isolated communities during winter using skis.

Earlier life

Jon Torsteinsson Rue, as he was then called, was born in the village of Tinn in the Telemark region of Norway in 1827. He lived on a farm that produced barely enough food to feed a large family of twelve children and two adults. When Jon was two years old his father died and unfortunately the family was obliged to vacate the farm. This happened at a time of many challenges in Norway where the majority of farmers were facing economic difficulties, not least because of the country's testing climate with its severe winters and wet summers. Such conditions made growing crops and keeping livestock a constant struggle.

Through the long Norwegian winters, skis were crafted from wood and used as the main form of transportation across the snow-covered rural landscape; they became lifesavers during those cold months. As soon as a child could walk, they were given a pair of skis and learned how to balance, manoeuvre and ski up and down hills. Like other children in Norway, Jon became proficient.

Unfortunately, after Jon's father died in 1829 providing enough food for a large family became even more arduous. The family managed to hold out until 1837 then his mother, Jon and more than fifty others from the immediate area took the difficult decision to migrate to the United States. They believed it was their best option if they wished to survive; hopefully, they would find new opportunities in this new land.

After making their way to Skein on the south Norwegian coast, they sailed to Gothenburg in Sweden before boarding the ship *Njord,* which took them to New York.

<u>Migration to a new land</u>

When they reached the United States, the family journeyed west, staying at locations where other Norwegians had previously settled. Like most migrants, they tried their hand at any type of work they could. They moved frequently, first to Chicago and then to a farm in Illinois. After that they travelled to Missouri then Iowa, after which Jon went to stay with his brother Torstein in Wisconsin.

It was around this time that Jon Torsteinsson Rue Americanised his name to 'John Thompson'. As with other non-English speaking migrants of the period, this was considered easier to handle in a predominantly Anglophile society. He developed a variety of manual skills including farm labouring, wood-cutting, well-digging and carpentry, but the discovery of gold in California tempted him, like so many others, to journey further west and make his fortune.

In the spring of 1851, 24-year-old John left for California. He and his brother Torstein drove a herd of milking cows as far as Placerville, California, just to the west of the Sierra Nevada Mountains, planning to sell milk to the many gold-diggers in the region.

Not long after his arrival in California, John also succumbed to the lure of the gold rush. He worked in three different mines and was also employed to build sawmills, together with other labouring jobs. By 1854 he had saved enough to buy a small farm in Putah Creek near Placerville.

When winter arrived, it brought a problem for those living near the mountains. The region was renowned for the huge amounts of snow that fell every winter which made travelling a significant problem; this was especially true for those living on the eastern side of the Sierras where residents were cut off for six months of the year as soon as the snow began to fall! This brought a real sense of isolation, especially as mail deliveries became practically impossible.

A few pioneering souls had tried to solve the problem and attempted to cross the Sierras' snow-filled mountain passes that rose as high as 2,800 metres. One man's effort had taken 60 days, which was too long to make a mail service viable. Somebody else had the idea of beating down the snow to make a track that would allow pack animals to walk without sinking, but sadly it didn't work. Another person used woven Canadian snowshoes to walk over the mountains; it took him eight days and unfortunately he was badly frozen during his attempt. Another couple took 16 days to cross the mountains using horses but their animals died in the freezing conditions. The task appeared to be impossible.

The residents of the region were desperate. The situation came to a head in 1855 when a local newspaper, *The Sacramento Union*, placed an advertisement:

'People Lost to the World; Uncle Sam Needs a Mail Carrier. People living east of the Sierra Nevada Mountains...lose contact with the outside world as winter snows cut off all communication. The greatest cry from the people is for mail.'

Reading this, John thought he might have a solution. He quietly set to work.

John 'Snowshoe' Thompson

John started making a pair of cross-country skis similar to those he had used as a child in Norway, believing that these might hold the key to travelling over the snow-covered mountains.

In North America during the mid-1800s, skis as such were not often used; they had only just been introduced, mostly by Scandinavian migrants. When people needed help to traverse thick snow, they occasionally used Canadian or Native American woven snowshoes. On the rare occasion skis were seen, they were so unusual that locals didn't even have a name for them and referred to them as 'snow-skates' or 'snowshoes'.

John started making his skis by cutting two strong pieces of oak about three metres in length, which he then turned up to a point at the front. They were around 10 centimetres wide, tapering to nine centimetres at the back, and about four centimetres thick. The resulting skis were hefty items weighing approximately 11 kilograms with a flat base and a single leather strap near to the centre for attaching a boot.

After constructing his skis, John stole away to some nearby snow and put in some serious practice before applying for the job of mailman. He had to convince people that it was feasible for him to ski across the mountains, especially after so many others had failed. Going uphill and along the flat, he could move the skis forward by taking small steps; he had to take upward gradients at a shallow incline or the skis simply slipped backwards. He carried a two-metre pole to punt himself along the flat and uphill. However, when travelling downhill, it was an entirely different story because it was relatively easy to rapidly gain speed. With great skill and deft movements, he kept such fast descents in check by using the pole and dragging it into the snow if necessary.

After a number of days practising, John was ready to present his method of winter mail delivery across the Sierras. When he demonstrated his movements up and down in the snow he travelled so fast downhill that,

> ...a few of his old friends among the miners...[were] swearing roundly that he would dash his brains out against a tree...

In no time at all, John had discovered his Nordic rhythm and flew down the steep mountainside holding his long pole horizontally like a tightrope walker. On other occasions he swayed it from side to side *'as a soaring eagle dips its wings'*.

John Thompson was given the job. One morning in early January 1855, a lone figure on a pair of long wooden skis carrying a heavy load headed eastwards towards the mountains. Locals watched and wondered what state he would be in on his return – if he ever returned! One onlooker called out, *'Good luck, Snowshoe Thompson!'*, which is how he got his nickname.

After only a few days, John skied back to Placerville looking none the worse for wear. People were amazed! So began his twice-a-month journey through the winter whenever the snows fell deep over the Sierras. The 145-kilometre trek from Placerville in California to the Carson Valley (in what is now Nevada) took three days out and two days back. His mailsack weighed anything between 27 and 45 kilograms; he carried an array of items including mail, newspapers, medicines, books, tools, cooking utensils and the occasional personal requests for people he knew en route. During his time as winter mailman, John also carried the first silver-ore samples that had been found in mines for analysis before the silver mine boom began.

He took very few personal belongings: his bag was heavy enough. Wearing only a wide-brimmed hat and a thick woollen jacket, John was warm enough as he skied along in the snow. He carried no camping gear, not even a blanket; if he wanted to rest at night he simply built a large fire and slept on a bed of pine with his feet towards it.

He never cooked any food during his journeys, preferring to eat dried beef, sausage, crackers and biscuits. When he wanted a drink he found a mountain stream or simply scooped up a handful of snow. There were occasions when he stayed in isolated cabins belonging to people he knew along the way; there were other times, especially if the snow was falling heavily, when he sheltered in caves or under rocky overhangs.

This six-foot-tall, blond, bearded, Norse-featured man, with charcoal smeared on his cheeks to prevent snow-blindness, felt at home in the mountains. He was often asked about getting lost, as he never carried a compass. His reply was, *'If you have your wits about you, there is never any danger of getting lost.'* He simply found his way by looking at the trees, rocks, snowdrifts, the way the streams flowed, the animal tracks he saw and by looking at the stars during the night.

But what about hungry mountain creatures such as grizzly bears, cougars and wolves? John refused to take a gun to defend himself because that would have meant carrying additional weight. Throughout his many winters of mountain skiing, he only had one close call with wild creatures when he encountered a pack of wolves devouring a deer carcass. When he saw them, he remained cool and continued skiing without slowing down. The six wolves stopped eating, left their meal and ran towards him before stopping some 20 metres away. Suddenly, the pack began howling in unison! As nonchalantly as he could, John stuck to his course and sped past. Expecting the pack to give chase, he was surprised when he looked back to see them continuing to eat the carcass.

John became widely known for his generosity and willingness to help others, particularly when he found people lost. On one of his journeys he encountered three exhausted men who had been caught in a ferocious storm. He rescued them one at a time by each standing on the back of his skis and placing their arms around him. After skiing downhill to safety, he returned for the next one; after repeating the rescue three times, John had skied a total of 90 extra kilometres, half of which with an extra person upon his skis!

Undoubtedly John's most celebrated rescue was during a journey in December 1856 when he stopped at an isolated cabin and found James Sisson, who had been out in a blizzard. The man was in a terrible state and had been lying alone for twelve days suffering from frostbite in his feet and with nothing to eat but raw flour. After building a fire to warm the man, John skied to the Carson Valley to find help. He returned with several others and together they built a makeshift sled to carry James to a doctor back in the valley. To save his life, the doctor proclaimed James' legs would need amputating because of their gangrenous condition – but he had no anaesthetic.

John skied 145 kilometres over the mountains to Placerville, then 80 more kilometres to Sacramento. Eventually, after obtaining some anaesthetic, he travelled back to Carson Valley. The injured man had his operation, which saved his life, after John had skied more than 650 kilometres in 10 days!

It was after this heroic event that fame really took hold and he became a legend in the mountains. Commenting on the extraordinary rescue, the postmaster at the time proclaimed:

'Most remarkable man I ever knew was John Thompson. He must be made of iron. Besides he never thinks of himself, but he'd give his last breath for anyone else - even a total stranger.'

John continued with his mail service in all weather conditions for twenty winters. As wagon trails slowly improved through the Sierras, he experimented by transporting mail using a sleigh pulled by horses wearing customised snowshoes. However, when the conditions were too severe he went back to carrying the mail by ski. When it wasn't winter, John worked on his new farm near Genoa to the east of the Sierras where he grew wheat, oats and potatoes, and looked after his own cattle and horses and those of his neighbours.

With the arrival of the transcontinental railroad in 1869, the need for a trans-Sierra winter mail service gradually diminished. However, John continued to deliver post on his skis to individuals during times of deep snow for some time to come.

Later years

In 1866 John became a United States citizen and married Agnes Singleton; the following year they had a son, Arthur. As time moved on, he also taught the local inhabitants how to both make and use skis.

Snowshoe Thompson is sometimes referred to as the 'father' of American skiing. Ski races and clubs first appeared in the United States during the 1860s, encouraged not least by John's skiing prowess. These early races, in which he occasionally took part, were mostly in the gold-rush settlements of the North Sierras. The races ran straight downhill and the prizes were pure silver dollars or bags of gold dust. It was calculated that John once sped downhill at 90 kph and completed 54-metre jumps on skis!

John started to represent his immediate area in local government. Eventually it emerged that during all the time he had been delivering the winter mail, he had not been paid by the US

Postal Service. It was suggested that he should visit the United States capital and ask for his back pay, and he carried a petition to that effect. Ironically, the train he was travelling on got stuck in a snowdrift. Determined as ever, John decided to walk 160 kilometres through the snow for three days until he could board another eastbound train.

After spending some days in Washington trying to obtain his back pay, it was discovered that John had never actually signed a contract so he wasn't entitled to any pay for his twenty winters of work! However, in 1975, almost 100 years after his death, the US Government finally compensated the skiing mailman; the money was used to build a memorial to the legendary skier.

John died in 1876 at the age of 49 from acute appendicitis followed by pneumonia. It was the end of a formidable life in which he had migrated to the New World and taken every opportunity to improve his circumstances. His extraordinary feats when skiing across the Sierra Mountains have become part of North American folklore, and most people would agree that John 'Snowshoe' Thompson has to be amongst the greatest skiers of all time.

'Welcome to Placerville' with a picture of Snowshoe Thompson

Old carriage and a pair of John's skis

Placerville in the winter during the gold rush

Snowshoe Thompson carrying his large rucksack (Credit: Smithsonian National Postal Museum)

*Snowshoe Thompson sliding downhill with pole
(Credit:Western American Ski Sport Museum)*

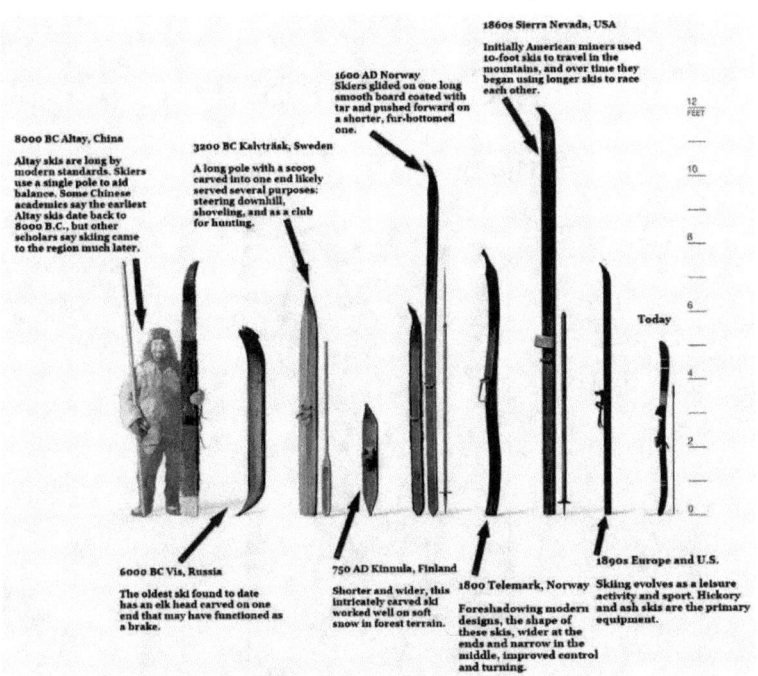

The history of skis. The 1860s Sierra Nevada skis are the longest! (Credit: Free the Powder Gloves)

Chapter 5

The Duke of the Abruzzi

Duke of the Abruzzi

The Duke and the rest of the ten strong climbing team, unfurled their Italian flag amidst immense jubilation.

The Duke of the Abruzzi was a member of the Savoy Royal Family, a mountaineer, explorer, African agriculturalist and an Italian admiral. He was a man of many talents who displayed a great deal of skill, passion and determination in his numerous adventures.

Early life

He was born in 1873, the third of Amadeo I of Spain's four sons; his mother was Maria Vittoria dal Pozzo. A few weeks after his birth his father was forced to abdicate the Spanish throne and his family moved to Italy.

Duke Luigi Amedeo of the Abruzzi, as he became known, was educated in Italy. Following royal tradition, he entered the Italian navy and his entire education took place in military school. He began as a ship's boy, quickly rising through the ranks to midshipman, and eventually commanded a frigate. The Duke sailed extensively around the world; when visiting foreign ports he sometimes represented the Italian royal family during formal events.

When he was not at sea, Luigi took to climbing mountains in the Alps. This became his passion and he completed numerous successful ascents including Monte Rosa, Mont Blanc, Gran Paradiso, Dente Blanche, Zinalrothorn, Grandes Jorasses and the difficult Zmutt Ridge on the Matterhorn. He had many other successful climbs, including the first ascent of Aiguille Petigax in the Mont Blanc massif.

Mount Saint Elias, Alaska

In 1897 the Duke, aged 24, led an expedition to North America to climb Mount Saint Elias, situated on the Canadian/Alaskan border. It was an unclimbed mountain and stood at 5489 metres in height. A number of climbers had attempted it before but had failed. The mountain had a reputation for unpredictable weather including continual mist, rain, sleet, snow and high winds, which often resulted in avalanches and stone fall.

After a lot of research and planning, the Duke was ready to make his attempt. The expedition consisted of four Italian guides he had climbed with previously, a doctor, a photographer, a number of other skilled assistants and ten American porters.

After landing in Yakutat Bay, the route took them through forests infested with mosquitoes before they could begin their journey by crossing the Malaspina Glacier. Using sledges, the party hauled their supplies across the ice of this massive glacier with its vast numbers of crevasses and seracs. It was exhausting work, requiring two men to pull and two to push each sledge, and the continual mist made navigating a suitable route even more of a problem.

The expedition battled for more than a month but eventually managed to cross the length of the Malaspina Glacier and reach the Seward, Agassiz and Newton Glaciers. Fortunately the weather improved on the dangerous Newton Glacier and eventually they reached the summit. The Duke and the rest of the ten-strong climbing team unfurled their Italian flag amidst immense jubilation.

The North Pole expedition

The Duke's next adventure was an attempt to be the first person to reach the North Pole. It was an opportunity to combine both his naval skills and his North American experience on Mount Saint Elias. During his preparations he was influenced by the expeditions carried out by Norwegian polar adventurer, Fridtjof Nansen. Like Nansen, the Duke decided to use sledges, dogs and similar equipment for his Arctic journey.

To test his equipment and gain further experience, the Duke travelled to Siberia and to Spitzbergen to train with some of his proposed expedition team members.

Finally, in 1899 at the age of 26, the Duke's North Pole expedition sailed north. They stopped briefly at Archangel in Russia to pick up 121 Siberian huskies. Their ship, *Stella Polare*, had sufficient food and supplies for the Italian expedition team, the Norwegian ship's crew and for the dogs for four years.

Through ever increasing frozen sea-ice, they sailed as far as Prince Rudolph Island where they anchored for the winter. After setting up camp on the island, their ship was damaged in the frozen sea. After successfully repairing her, the Italians started practising driving their sledges across the ice to prepare for the journey to the Pole. During one such session the Duke damaged his fingers after his sledge crashed; his hand was frostbitten and so badly damaged that several fingers needed to be partially amputated.

Due to this unfortunate mishap, he was forced to stay behind when the Italian sledging party left for the North Pole. A total of thirteen sledges, 104 dogs and three teams of four men set off. In charge was Umberto Cagni, who had been with the Duke on many of his previous adventures. The idea was that, as they journeyed further towards their goal, some in the party would return and leave the stronger members to travel to the top of the world.

From the outset the expedition experienced extremely difficult terrain, including huge blocks of ice and open water; consequently, the distances they travelled each day were far shorter than planned. After some of the team had accidents and some were frostbitten, they all returned to Prince Rupert Island.

Adjustments were made to clothing and equipment before they set off on their next attempt. Just as before, they faced tough conditions with overnight temperatures dropping to as low as minus 47 degrees Celsius.

Cagni calculated how much food they would need to complete their journey to the North Pole and, after assessing the situation, sent back two teams. He pressed ahead, eventually achieving a latitude of 86 degrees, 34 minutes North, a new 'farthest north' record! At that point the last team returned, only just managing to get back to base in the extremely hazardous conditions.

Arriving back on Prince Rupert Island, they discovered that one of the earlier groups, a team of three led by Lieutenant Francesco Queerini, hadn't returned. It was assumed that the trying terrain, difficult navigation, lack of food supplies and possibly an accident might have led to their absence.

Using explosives, the remaining adventurers freed the *Stella Polare* from the ice, where it had been trapped for a year, and eventually the ship returned to Norway. The Duke arranged rescue attempts to find the three missing expedition members but to no avail.

As well as achieving a new northerly latitude record, the expedition had managed to successfully carry out a range of scientific studies.

The Ruwenzori Mountains

In 1906, the Duke turned his attention to the Ruwenzori Mountains, sometimes referred to as the Mountains of the Moon. The second-century geographer Ptolemy was one of the first to mention these white-topped East African mountains. The Ruwenzori peaks (today spelt 'Rwenzori') were believed to be the source of the River Nile, though nobody was certain.

This little-known mountain range is situated some 32 kilometres north of the Equator on the border between Uganda and what was then the Belgian Congo. The mountains cover an area some 50 kilometres by 130 kilometres. Previous expeditions had failed to explore and climb all of the range because of its challenging terrain and poor weather conditions.

The Duke decided to organise a large expedition with some 300 people, including climbers, a military escort, about 200 porters, caravan leaders, servants and other assistants.

As the party approached the Ruwenzori Mountains they faced many problems as they made their way through the dense rainforest but eventually they established a base camp near to the Mobuku Glacier. Unlike previous parties to the Ruwenzori, the Duke and his team were fortunate in having a period of settled and clear weather. At different times, members succeeded in climbing all sixteen of the major peaks in the range, including the highest, the Margherita Peak at 5,109 metres.

The expedition carried-out extensive scientific studies, which included discovering that the Ruwenzori mountain range was not the main source of the River Nile but one of a number feeding that great river. The expedition had been a resounding success.

Karakorum Expedition

In 1909, the Duke gained permission to climb K2 and explore the Baltoro Glacier in the Karakoram Mountains. His aim was to make a first ascent and, in doing so, achieving a new world altitude record.

K2 stood at 8,611 metres and was a formidable mountain to climb; others had tried to climb it but none had been successful. The logistics in ascending such a towering peak with its extreme weather, was another huge undertaking, so once again the Duke assembled a group of friends from his previous trips together with others who had particularly useful expertise. Members included those skilled in mountaineering, photography, medicine and science.

Thinking about the task ahead of them, the Duke designed new tents that could withstand both cold and hot conditions. He also created a new four-layer sleeping bag to use on the mountain.

After arriving at the Baltoro Glacier, they established different camps as they made their way up K2. The continual snowy conditions resulted in numerous avalanches; to avoid these, the climbers decided to follow the ridge with the least snow on it, which eventually became known as the Abruzzi Spur.

After some time they reached a high point of 6,700 metres, some way short of their goal, so they decided to try a different route up the mountain – but once again they met with extremely deep snow. Their high point on this attempt was 6,666m.

Accepting the challenging conditions on K2, but not yet ready to give up, they turned their attention to the lower peak, Staircase Peak (today called Skyang Kangri). Once again they were forced to retreat after experiencing poor conditions. They then moved to

Chogolisa, another unclimbed summit at 7,668 metres. As had become the pattern, challenging conditions slowed their progress and sometimes the climbers found themselves waist deep in snow. Although they didn't succeed in getting to the summit, they climbed to 7,500 metres, a new world altitude record.

It was yet another successful expedition; furthermore, the Duke's scientific observations had proved that it was possible to live for many days above 6,400 metres.

Later years

During World War One, the Duke became the commander-in-chief of the Italian fleet. He left the navy in 1917, after which he spent most of his time in Italian Somaliland. He built an experimental agricultural community about 90 kilometres north-east of Mogadishu, where both Italian migrants and local Somalis shared in the benefits of new agricultural methods. This became a huge project involving the construction of a new dam, irrigation channels, new roads, a railway and canals. The community, called the Duke of Abruzzi Village, also had shops, a cinema, a hospital, schools, factories, a mosque and a church; by 1928 3,000 Somalis and 200 Italians were living and working there. During this time the Duke married a Somali woman called Faduma Ali and they made their home in the village.

In 1928, the Duke organised a local East African expedition to find the source of the river known as Webi-Shebella, which flowed through this new agricultural centre. He and his expedition team travelled some 1,400 kilometres following the river and located its source, after which the area was duly mapped. The expedition also carried out a range of investigations that were useful for future agricultural and economic development.

The Duke of Abruzzi died in 1933 at the age of 60 years in his village in Italian Somalia. So ended a life of extraordinary adventures over a range of terrain across the world. His incredible journeys to extreme locations made him one of the most significant adventurers of that pioneering era.

Duke Luigi Amedeo of the Abruzzi

Faduma Ali, the Duke's wife

K2 on the 1909 expedition (Credit:Vittorio Sella)

The Stella Polare in Arctic waters

Chapter 6

Thomas Hiram Holding

Thomas Holding

Singlehandedly, Thomas had opened up the idea of people going off and enjoying camping adventures

Thomas Hiram Harding is considered to be the father of modern-day camping. He was a tailor by profession, a participant in a range of outdoor pursuits, a lifelong camper, a designer of camping equipment and a writer of books about camping. His enthusiasm and expertise inspired many people to take up camping during the turn of the last century.

Early life

Thomas was born in 1844 into a large family of eight in the village of Prees in Shropshire. His parents became Mormon converts, which influenced their decision to leave Britain and emigrate to America. On reaching their new land, they had to spend five weeks camping on the banks of the Mississippi River before they could join a wagon train heading west.

My first experience of camping was above the wooded slope on the plateau behind the Mississippi, when a lad of nine. There, 300 of us camped in tents and wagons, which camp lasted for about five weeks.

Once their journey was underway, every night was spent camping out. It was under the wide skies of North America that Thomas developed a passion for outdoor life. Each day was an open-air education as he travelled on his wagon train learning the skills and nuances of a life permanently on the move. For this young boy, it was an incredible experience, as he once reflected:

The plains were then uninhabited save for a few wandering tribes [of Native Americans], probably a million antelopes, and possibly half-a-million of wary buffaloes. Soon afterwards, this gallant herd was swept away before the 'railway hunger', i.e. they were shot by Buffalo Bill and others to feed the hungry navvies who constructed the line.

The intention was to cross the American plains and mountains as far as Salt Lake City where the family would settle, a westward journey of around 2,000 kilometres. Unfortunately, like so many who decided to 'go west', their trip wasn't without hardship and tragedy. Along the way two of the eight Harding children died, and Thomas once fell under a wagon weighing a *'ton-and-a-quarter'*, the wheels of which ran over the small of his back. Thankfully he survived, but the loss of two children inflicted tremendous sorrow on the family.

Adding to their grief, word reached them when they arrived in Salt Lake City that Thomas's grandfather had died. Abandoning their dream of a new life, the family joined another wagon train heading back from where they had just travelled.

Once again they were subjected to a perilous journey over the Rocky Mountains and across wide plains, during which time another young child was born. After this second wagon train journey, they returned to Britain.

When he was a little older, Thomas started learning the tailoring trade as he travelled to various locations throughout the country. In 1869 he married his wife, Sarah, and during the following years they had four sons and one daughter.

Camping in the British Isles

Even though his experiences crossing America had been a mixture of both delight and sadness, Thomas retained a great love for the outdoors. Although he and his growing family moved to different areas of the country for his tailoring work, whenever possible he found time to escape into the countryside.

He became a keen supporter of the 'Muscular Christianity' movement whose ideals advocated a wholesome, athletic and disciplined lifestyle. A key element of their beliefs was to take regular exercise, which Thomas did by sailing, canoeing and cycling.

As a keen cyclist, in 1878 he formed the Bicycle Touring Club, which later became the Cyclists' Touring Club. Around this time, he went on a canoeing and camping trip in the Scottish Highlands. During the journey he carried bulky equipment in his vessel so he could camp overnight along the way. He wrote a book about his experience entitled, *The Cruise of the Osprey*.

A few years later Thomas enjoyed another camping and canoeing trip in Scotland and wrote a book entitled *Watery Wanderings in Western Lochs*. From his interest in canoeing, he helped set up and became a founding member of the British Canoe Association.

Thomas was always thinking about the craft of camping and how it could be made more practical and easier. There was the eternal problem of the equipment being heavy and cumbersome; due to the weight involved, an excursion always required something like a canoe or dinghy to transport camping gear.

During the 1880s there was a bicycle boom, which provided an opportunity for people to travel a little further. Those who could afford these new machines could go out and explore the world beyond their immediate surroundings. 'Safety cycles', as their name suggests, were easier to ride and less dangerous than earlier 'ordinary cycles' such as the penny farthing. These new machines had the same size wheels and a chain drive to the rear wheel, where the riders' feet could touch the ground. Later models even had pneumatic tyres and brakes! As a result, cycling grew in popularity.

In the 1890s Thomas, together with his son and two friends, went bicycle-camping in Ireland; this is believed to be the very first cycle and camping trip. For their journey Thomas devised a custom-made, simple ridge tent constructed from a single sheet of canvas. He used sticks to secure it to the ground and tensioned it with a rope.

In 1897, Thomas wrote another book describing their trip, *Cycle and Camp in Connemara*. The publication created interest in many quarters and numerous people contacted him to find out more about the pleasures of cycling and camping.

On the back of such interest, Thomas decided to form the Association of Cycle Campers in 1901. Their first meeting had thirteen members in attendance, but the number had risen to several hundred by 1906. In the same year, Thomas also launched another camping group, The National Camping Club, which added yet more individuals to the movement. In just over a year the new group numbered some 250 members, with *'hundreds more pursuing the sport unaffiliated'*.

Camping as a mass movement

To help those seeking a camping life, Thomas decided to write another book called *The Camper's Handbook*. Published in 1908, it described the basics of camping and covered a wide range of topics to guide the budding camper. Thomas wanted to share the knowledge and skills he had acquired over the years.

There were sections on how to set-up camp in various kinds of terrain; what types of tent to use; what food to take and how to cook it; how to organise the inside of a tent; sleeping arrangements, and the clothes to wear when camping. The book was packed with advice and helpful tips – there was even a description of the methods available for transporting camping gear by canoe, dinghy, cycle, horse-drawn caravan or by foot. Finally, at the end of the handbook there was a list of campsites throughout the land. In short, it was a comprehensive manual for all campers, whether they were just starting out or were familiar hands. This handbook transformed Thomas into the greatest authority on camping and it became a 'must-have' for all enthusiasts.

As a tailor by profession, Thomas found it relatively straightforward to create his own tent designs, including his lightweight silk tent, the 'Wigwam Tent', that could be folded and carried in a pocket. Walking sticks could be used as the Wigwam poles with only the iron pegs having any real weight.

He also developed a lighter pressure-paraffin cooking stove he named the Baby Primus. However, one of his greatest designs was the Thomas Holding Lightweight Bike Kit. The emphasis was on making the kit as light as possible, and a central feature was an oiled-silk tent weighing just 312 grammes, with 425 grammes telescopic bamboo poles. The kit had a down-quilt of 680 grammes and a baby primus that clipped onto the cycle.

Thomas was a practical person: when he saw a problem with any camping equipment, he simply redesigned it. An example was his Campo Milk Tin, a container that transported milk without leaking. Then there was the Canadian Sack, a one- or two-strap rucksack, depending on preference, for people who wanted to spend time in isolated mountainous regions where supplies would have to be carried over considerable distances.

Thomas decided there was a problem with horse-drawn caravans of the time: to move one required *'too much horse to drag it about!'* No doubt drawing upon his boyhood experiences of travelling by wagon train across America, he designed a lightweight caravan weighing just under 550 kilograms, much less than the much heavier ones that were currently being used. In his handbook there was a page of plans and dimensions for his lighter caravan.

The Camper's Handbook is full of intriguing glimpses into the camping and caravanning world of the time; it is also an historical document that looks into societal diktats and what was acceptable in the early 1900s.

Singlehandedly, Thomas had opened up the idea of people enjoying camping adventures anywhere in the British countryside. Before the 1880s, people who camped did so largely out of necessity; now people could camp for pleasure and for wholesome exercise and relaxation.

Later years

After the First World War, the camping movement continued to evolve and increase in popularity. The concept of camping fed into the Government's 'healthy living and lifestyle' promotions, which were steadily unfolding in an attempt to encourage the nation into wholesome practices. It was believed that escaping the squalor of cities and occasionally getting out into the great outdoors to enjoy fishing, hunting and camping helped to develop greater moral, physical and spiritual well-being. Thomas wrote:

Camping spread across the classes and professions. Almost every division into which society in England is split has contributed to the ranks of the camping fraternity today.

The enthusiasm for camping showed no signs of abating: Thomas's recreational revolution was here to stay. He continued to work as a tailor during weekdays but come the weekend he escaped into the countryside and went camping. His passion remained as strong as ever.

Thomas Harding died in 1930 at his home in London at the age of 86.

Today, many thousands of people up and down the land enjoy camping. Such enthusiasm can be directly traced back to Thomas Hiram Holding, the father of modern day camping!

'Baby Primus' and the 'So-Soon' pan invented by Thomas

Cover of 'Cycle and Camp in Connemara' by T.H. Holding

Sleeping bag illustration from 'The Camper's Handbook'

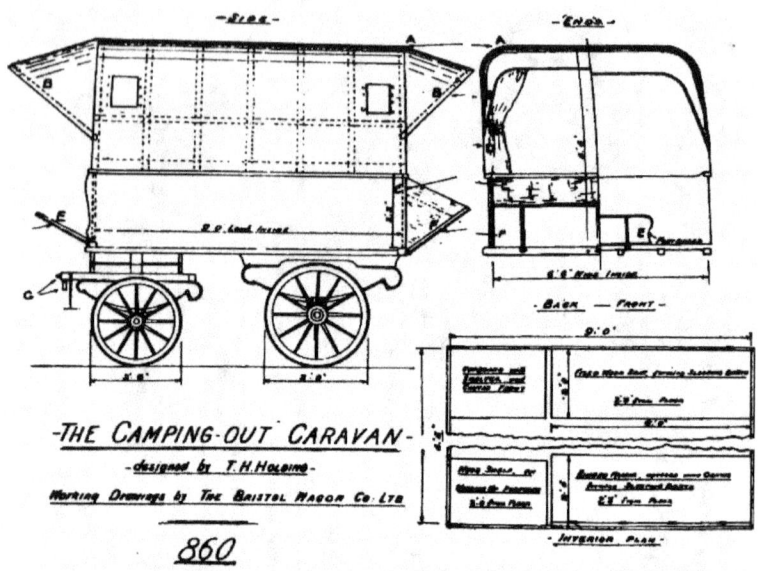

The 'Camping-out Caravan' designed by Thomas

The 'Thomas Holding Lightweight Bike Kit'

The 'Canadian Sack'

Thomas 'canoe-camping'

Thomas next to his 312 gramme silk tent

Chapter 7

William Sachtleben   Thomas Allen

William Sachtleben and Thomas Allen

Just three years…lacking twenty days, we rolled into New York on our wheels, having put a girdle around the earth.

William Sachtleben and Thomas Allen were adventurers from the United States famed for cycling around the world between 1890 and 1893.

<u>Early life</u>

William was born in 1866 and Thomas in 1868 in the USA. As fortune would have it, they both attended Washington University in Saint Louis in the state of Missouri. Whilst there, they became friends after realising that they both had a passion for adventure. As well as completing their studies, the pair planned a bicycle tour that would take place after they finished university. Such an adventure would enable them to experience the 'real world', and it would be a perfect way to round off their academic education.

Round the world on a bicycle

William and Thomas decided to complete their tour using the newly invented 'safety bicycles', the popular successor to penny-farthings. During their trip they intended to meet local people without using guides or interpreters. William said:

We love to roam on our bicycles, unfettered, amongst the scenes of unsophisticated nature and the common people.

They planned to ride together because it would be safer than travelling alone; they would be able to *'watch each other's backs'*. The initial idea was to visit a few destinations within Europe so, with their plans made quite literally the day after completing their university courses, they began their journey. William's father, knowing his son's hunger for adventure, said, *'Well, son, stay away until you get your fill.'*

After sailing across the Atlantic they arrived in Liverpool in July 1890 and purchased 18 kilogram safety cycles with a single gear, hard-tyres and no brakes. With an additional seven kilograms of items strapped to the handlebars, they cycled across Wales, over to Ireland and on into Scotland. It was only when overnighting in Galashiels in Scotland that they hit upon the idea of cycling around the entire globe. They were enjoying themselves, so why not keep going and encircle the world?

When they reached London, William and Thomas spent time organising their revised tour. William managed to strike a deal with a popular magazine, the *Penny Illustrated Paper*; to help cover costs, he agreed to send back regular reports throughout their journey. Also in London, the Iroquois Cycle Company provided them with new bicycles that had hollow rubber tyres, and they purchased a newly invented Kodak box camera that would enable them to make a visual record of their journey. Most importantly, they spent considerable time securing travel documentation from the Turkish, Persian, Russian and Chinese embassies so they could travel through potentially problematic and volatile regions.

With their new plans complete, they continued their journey through France and into Italy. Along the way they visited a number of cities, towns and regions where they absorbed the culture and geography, complementing what they had learned during their university days.

Whilst cycling through Europe, they were often accompanied by cyclists from cycling clubs. Bicycling was becoming extremely popular throughout the continent, and the American travellers were interviewed by cycling magazines that had sprung up across the continent.

Arriving in Greece, they made their way to Athens where they took a break after having travelled about 6,500 kilometres across Europe.

From Constantinople (Istanbul) the cyclists crossed the Bosporus and rode in an easterly direction across Asia. This was the beginning of the most challenging part of their journey. They attempted to cycle the wagon road to Ismid but switched to travelling along the track of a railway line, which greatly tested their skills. They were regularly confronted by locals who were wary of strangers; occasionally rocks were thrown at them and aggressive dogs often chased them.

In many areas the local authorities forced the pair to hire mounted armed guards to look after them. This was useful on some occasions, for example to help them cross deep rivers, but at other times it was a hindrance always having the guards around.

William and Thomas had to stay alert for problems; on one occasion William had the spokes in his wheel kicked in by a mule! As they continued, although always tired from a day's riding, they were obliged to provide a demonstration of cycling for the local audience that had invariably gathered.

Throughout their journey across Asia it was often the first time bicycles had been seen so, before eating or resting they showed how they were ridden to the great joy of onlookers. They always tried to listen to advice from people they met along the way, learned a smattering of the local language, were sensitive to customs and traditions and ate local food. However, during their ride across Turkey, they were forced to rest whilst Thomas recovered after having caught typhoid fever.

When he was fit again, they cycled to Bayazid where they planned to ascend Mount Ararat. After announcing their intentions, the adventurers met a degree of discouragement from local inhabitants who said that it would be too dangerous. A major concern were bands of locals who were known to take hostages in the region.

Not dissuaded, the determined pair had local craftspeople make them two alpenstocks and had large nails driven into the soles of their shoes to act as crampons. The Americans were joined by an elderly Austrian, Ignaz Raffl, who had been told about the foreigners on their 'devils' carts' who wished to climb Mount Ararat. With donkeys carrying supplies and two local guards, the party began their ascent.

By day two, the group consisted of just the Americans and the Austrian as they made their way upwards onto snow and steep terrain. After an uncomfortable overnight bivouac under a single blanket, they continued in freezing conditions over snow, ice and rocks. Using their alpenstocks, they slowly gained height until they finally reached the summit of Mount Ararat's peak at 5,137 metres, only the seventh party in history to do so.

After their triumph they entered Persia and crossed a dry landscape as they pedalled towards Teheran. Sections of their route were extremely difficult and sometimes the only way to make any progress was to push their bikes.

During this period it was William's turn to be attacked by typhoid fever, which put a halt to any cycling for several weeks. When he had recovered, they continued through barren hills, wasteland and desert in searing hot temperatures sometimes reaching 50 degrees Celsius in the shade.

In Teheran they waited for Russian permits that would enable them to continue. Eventually they entered the regions of Turkmenistan and Uzbekistan in the Russian Empire. At Tashkent in eastern Uzbekistan, they halted their journey during the winter months.

Although they were advised to continue their ride by staying within the Russian Empire, they made their way towards China. They travelled in a region of steppe and a wilderness of lakes and swamps that they described as having '...*an absence of landmarks with a boundless level expanse*'. The pair were often followed by local horsemen who were curious how they would cross the many streams and rivers that barred the way. Without any assistance, they cyclists forded these by wading through the water carrying their clothing and bicycles upon their shoulders.

After presenting their entry papers at the Chinese border, they rode to the town of Kuldja (today called Yining). Here they entertained a crowd of 3,000 onlookers with their cycle riding prowess, which ended in a race between them and local horsemen. However, a problem arose in this frontier town with their visas and money to use if they wanted to cross the rest of China. They eventually exchanged other currency that they had for pieces of silver that they concealed about their bicycles. While such problems were being ironed out, they spent their time learning as much of the Chinese language as possible.

After travelling through the Tien Shan Mountains, the Americans arrived at the city of Ürümqi. Their arrival had been eagerly anticipated; consequently one of the biggest crowds to date was waiting for them to demonstrate their cycling skills. William wrote in his notes:

They [the crowds] overcame the antipathy for the foreigner, and made us cordially welcome...our bicycles were after all our best passports.

Again, William and Thomas's careful planning had paid off. During various stretches of their Chinese journey, local people were only too willing to help them overcome a variety of challenges.

When they reached the oasis of Hami, they prepared to cross the Gobi Desert. *'...The great Gobi stretched out before us like a vast ocean of endless space.'* It was a region of red sand, wiry shrubs and strong winds. It was often too difficult to ride in the wind, which resulted in many hours of pushing their bikes. Overnight they stay in vermin-infested station houses made out of mud that had been specially built for travellers. Having to drink brackish water at these huts resulted in both of them suffering from upset stomachs, fevers and vomiting.

Eventually they overcame the hardships of the Gobi Desert and emerged into a far more fertile landscape with more vegetation, including grass and cultivated crops. There was water everywhere being used for irrigation as they made their way beside fields of rice, opium poppies and tea.

Unfortunately, during one rapid descent down a narrow pathway, a damaged pedal led to its complete disintegration and the cycle frame was entirely bent. After some makeshift repairs in the next settlement, they re-built the machine as best they could but it was barely rideable and had a waddling movement.

They continued towards Peking (Beijing) with greetings from dignitaries, meetings with missionaries and the usual demonstrations of their riding skills (now made more difficult with a somewhat wobbly cycle). After more than 11,000 kilometres of an Asian journey that most people had deemed impossible, they entered Peking. The riders wrote *'...our wheels and clothing were nearly in pieces'*.

Their extraordinary feat was celebrated in the English language newspaper, the *North China Herald*, and they were provided with fresh clothes to attend a rare, formal meeting with the Prime Minister of China, Li-Hung-Chang, during which they discussed their bicycle journey.

From Peking's seaport at Tientsin, William and Thomas boarded a ship to San Francisco where they disembarked. Victors Cycles donated two brand-new cycles before they set off on the final leg of their 'graduation trip' around the globe.

From California they cycled through Arizona, New Mexico and Texas before reaching William's home near St Louis in Illinois. Along the way they were often accompanied by many wheelman (cycling) club members who had learned about their worldwide tour, and they were celebrated as heroes.

In the spring of 1893, they arrived back in New York or, as the adventurers put it, *'Just three years…lacking twenty days, we rolled into New York on our wheels, having put a girdle around the earth'*. They had successfully completed a unique journey circumnavigating the globe by bicycle totalling a staggering 29,000 kilometres across three continents!

<u>After cycling around the world</u>

The adventurers found considerable acclaim after their journey. Their extraordinary achievement was celebrated across the United States, not least amongst fellow cyclists.

The pair went their separate ways. William opened a bicycle store in St Louis and tried his hand at cycle racing. He also dabbled in acting: he took a leading role in a production of *A Dream of Ancient Greece* at the Alton Theater in Illinois. However, after learning the news of the mysterious disappearance of another round-the-world American cyclist, Frank Lenz, he went to search for him.

Lenz's family and *Outing Magazine,* an American publication for which Frank was writing reports, had lost all contact with him in Turkey. William went to Constantinople and then to Erzurum, the last place Frank had been seen. On several occasions during his investigation, his life was in grave danger because of the instability in Turkey at that time. Eventually he concluded that Lenz had almost certainly been killed by Kurdish bandits.

Ever the adventurer, in 1900 William travelled to Cape Nome in north-western Alaska. There he prospected for gold as well as writing newspaper articles. In 1903 he married Mae Merriman and eventually moved to Houston, Texas where he ran the Majestic Theater. He died in 1953.

As for Thomas, he spent time writing about their global adventure and also presented a series of lectures that he illustrated with slide projections taken during their three-year journey. He became a correspondent with a newspaper syndicate and travelled across Siberia reporting on the Trans-Siberian Railway, which was under construction at the time.

After that he married Annie Mackay, a Scot, and became a British citizen. He stopped his adventuring and concentrated on developing an engineering business. Thomas had already displayed his engineering talents during his cycling trip; it has been suggested he was the main mechanic during their epic journey. During the following years he invented a water pump, a carbide lamp and a braking system for automobiles. His company eventually became a multinational corporation. He died in 1955.

William Sachtleben and Thomas Allen led interesting lives manifested by a host of varied experiences, but they will always be remembered for their daring and successful trip by bicycle around the world. This groundbreaking ride was the longest continuous bicycle journey ever recorded at the time, a truly unique trip and an inspiration for many future adventurers.

Crowds gathering to see William and Allen ride their cycles (Credit: Michael Perry)

Great Wall of China (Credit: Michael Perry)

Evening rest in a Turkish village (Credit: Michael Perry)

In the Gobi Desert (Credit: Michael Perry)

Chapter 8

Frank Samuelsen   *George Harbo*

George Harbo and Frank Samuelsen

It should be possible for two good men in a good boat to row across the ocean.

George Harbo and Frank Samuelsen were the first people to row across an ocean when, in 1896, they rowed across the North Atlantic from New York to the Scilly Isles.

Their early lives

George Harbo was born in 1864 in the village of Brevik in rural south-east Norway. Like many young men at the time, he decided to leave his native land because the country was finding it difficult to support a sudden growth in its population. He migrated to the United States where he found a place to live on the New Jersey coast together with other new Norwegian arrivals and worked as a crewman aboard a small fishing boat. After a year, he had earned enough money to sail back to Norway and marry his betrothed, Anine, then return to America.

Frank Samuelsen was born in 1870 near the coastal town of Farsund in southern Norway. He grew up on a small farm that produced grain and potatoes as well as keeping dairy cows. He also took the opportunity to seek a different life for himself and signed on as a merchant seaman, sailing to the West Indies, South America, Africa and the west coast of the United States. This tall, physically imposing man soon held the position of bosun's mate and encouraged his fellow sailors to sail at full speed whenever it was required. After six years, Frank began to think about an alternative life for himself so in 1893 he bade farewell to his ship in New York. Like many other Norwegian migrants, he also made his way to the fishing villages of New Jersey.

On his return to the United States, George had settled in the same area as before with his new wife and son. As well as fishing, he also worked as a harbour pilot, guiding vessels in and out of New York harbour. It was challenging and exacting work, which he was well qualified to do having studied advanced navigation back in Norway. George also built a rowing boat that he took out to sea to collect clams.

He and Frank eventually met and became good friends. They decided to join forces in search of clams and went to sea day after day and in all weathers. George and his wife had two more children but, due to an economic downturn in the United States, Anine and the three children moved back to Norway.

George and Frank continued their clamming work off the coast of New Jersey. During long periods in the boat together, the two men learned each other's moods and capabilities. Each day they rowed many kilometres to search for the molluscs, extract them, and place them on the boat before returning. The work was routine and uneventful but provided enough of a living to see them through the nation's economic slump.

It was during one such day that George revealed to Frank an idea that he had been considering for some time: *'I've been thinking, Frank. It should be possible for two good men in a good boat to row across the ocean.'*

Frank's immediate response was to laugh but when he realised his friend was serious, they began to discuss the feasibility of such a journey. Taking a small vessel across an ocean had never been attempted before, and there were many potential problems and dangers to consider.

George was convinced that with a well-designed craft, using the summer westerly winds, and by reaching the Gulf Stream to help them on their way, it could be done. What's more, if they succeeded the two men would become rich and famous. Many people in both Europe and North America would want to hear such an adventurous tale.

Although Frank had many doubts about George's idea, the seed had been sown and over time it became a regular topic of conversation. With continuing economic problems, prospects for both men appeared to be somewhat limited in their adopted country.

George and Frank decided to forge ahead with their dream, concluding, like many other great adventurers, that they really had nothing to lose. Eventually, and with some trepidation, they shared the idea with their families who were, as they had anticipated, not over-enthusiastic.

Anine now had another child, conceived after George had made a brief return to Norway, though sadly one of their other children had died. Frank's family, some of whom were also living in the United States, were equally doubtful about their success.

Undaunted, the pair pressed ahead and tried to secure sponsorship for the many costs that would be involved. Unfortunately nothing was forthcoming apart from the editor of the popular nationwide newspaper, *The Police Gazette,* who promised them medals and some publicity in exchange for the boat being named after the paper's owner, Mr Richard Fox.

Lacking financial support, the pair continued to work hard and put all their hard-earned cash and savings into buying provisions for the journey. Their greatest expense was the construction of a new boat that needed to be built carefully with features that would cope with some very challenging seas.

The craft was made by one of the best local boat builders. *The Fox,* as it was to be called, was 5.5 metres in length and 1.5 metres wide, and constructed from oak and white cedar. Airtight compartments were built into it to help stop the boat from sinking. In addition, there were rails on the keel that could be used to right the craft if it were turned over during a storm. There were three sets of oars tethered to the boat at all times.

Stored away were more than 100 litres of fresh water, 45 kilograms of tinned biscuits, bags of coffee, tomatoes, onions and 250 eggs protected in seaweed. There were cans of corned beef, ham and roast beef, jars of jam and a few bottles of wine. They also had a compass, sextant, nautical almanac, charts, a log book and a kerosene stove. The provisions were to last for an estimated 60-day crossing and weighed as heavy as *The Fox* itself!

<u>Crossing the North Atlantic</u>

By June 6th, 1896, the intrepid oarsmen were ready to start rowing across the Atlantic Ocean towards Europe. George and

Frank sat in *The Fox* wearing woollen shirts, thick oilskin overalls, oilskin jackets and rubber boots. A crowd of more than 1,000 onlookers had gathered to witness the start of their historical journey, most of whom were sceptical about its success and many believing it was suicidal.

There were a number of official looking men in the crowd from influential newspapers who had come to certify that *The Fox* was indeed a rowing boat and was not equipped with a mast, sail or rudder; such official confirmation was necessary if a record for rowing across the Atlantic were to be established. If George and Frank encountered any ships as they crossed the ocean, these checks would be repeated.

Amidst cheers, applause, and with larger vessels blowing their whistles, George and Frank started rowing. The adventure had begun!

At the end of their first day at sea, they encountered both fog and rain. During the following day, the last traces of the American coastline were lost to the horizon. That night George and Frank began a routine of sharing overnight watches: one man kept rowing eastwards whilst the other slept upon reindeer cushions and blankets. The men alternated watches which were either two-and-a-half or three hours in length. The person rowing kept a lookout for lights from ships because any large vessel approaching too close required them to steer clear to avoid a collision.

A few days later, by using their sextant they worked out that they had rowed some 160 kilometres. After days of straightforward progress, the conditions suddenly changed and the men experienced stronger winds, turbulent water and huge waves. Both of them rowed through the night to fight the storm. As *The Fox* twisted, turned and rode the massive waves, they needed all their skill to stay afloat. Waves continually crashed into and over the little boat and one of the men had to continually bail out water. The storm tested George, Frank and *The Fox*!

As the conditions gradually eased, they were able to take stock. They were completely soaked, their muscles ached, their hands were numb from the cold, and they had deep, bleeding calluses on their palms and fingers. They hadn't been able to drink or eat anything for many hours, so they lit the kerosene stove to make some coffee – and it suddenly burst into flames along with the housing in which it was placed. Encouraged by the wind, the blaze gathered in strength and black smoke rose above the craft. They were able to extinguish the fire by dousing it with water; a potential tragedy had been averted!

The weather settled down after the storm and they made good progress, travelling around 150 kilometres in one 24-hour period. They were visited by a lone hammerhead shark, which, after swimming alongside for hours on end, simply disappeared. The pair also communicated with a passing ship whose captain asked if they needed any assistance. After explaining what they were doing, the rowers asked that their position be reported to the authorities so *The Fox*'s progress could be tracked.

On another night they encountered a second ship – but this time it was a much larger vessel and was heading straight towards them! By making a hurried turn of ninety degrees, and with both men literally rowing for their lives, they avoided being smashed to pieces.

The relatively settled seas gradually gave way to another developing storm. As a gale blew, huge waves struck *The Fox*, requiring one person to row as best they could with the other having to continually bail. The tiny craft swirled in the volatile sea, making progress impossible. The men hurriedly donned their reindeer-hair lifebelts and decided to deploy the 'floating anchor' they had brought with them. Dropping it into the water helped stabilise *The Fox*. The two men decided to sit at the bottom of the craft and simply ride out the turmoil. In time, they pulled in the sea anchor and continued rowing eastwards.

With greatly improved weather conditions, George and Frank travelled more than 200 kilometres in two days. They even risked lighting their stove again and enjoyed a hot drink, the first in many, many days.

Apart from developing calluses on their hands and buttocks, their circumstances had improved, though they were slightly concerned that the fifty or so whales that had decided to join them might overturn their boat. But, after a period of time, the whales swam away.

As the good weather conditions held, once again they made progress and on occasion covered up to 80 kilometres each day; however, the weather gradually deteriorated and there was no respite from the high seas, wind and cold, with little opportunity to rest, eat or drink. The wild weather continued, producing big swells to row through, sometimes between nine and 12 metres in height! The men were battered and bruised with trying to maintain direction, bailing and riding out this new storm. Finally, after battling for days, there was a definite lull in the wind one night and the temperature suddenly tumbled; they realised they were in the lee of an enormous iceberg! Rowing with extra vigour, they avoided its destructive force which could have easily crushed their boat.

Although the sea remained lively, the westerly winds pushed them eastwards. Their craft continued to be buffeted, with breakers continually swamping the vessel. Several times they almost capsized but their luck held – until the situation deteriorated with winds of 100–130 kilometres per hour. *The Fox* was being tossed in all directions. George and Frank couldn't hear each other shout in the roar of the maelstrom, then a huge wave struck them and the boat capsized. The two men were thrown into the water but luckily their life jacket tethers were connected to the boat and they managed to pull themselves onto the upturned *Fox*.

Amidst all the turmoil they managed to flip over *The Fox* using the specially designed rails beneath the craft. They leapt in and started bailing. Once again George and Frank had to quickly consider their situation. Half of their provisions had been lost, together with their cooking gear.

Although they were shivering uncontrollably after being submerged in the extremely cold water, they carried on rowing and eventually the storm abated. Having been without sleep and fighting the elements for three days, they were exhausted, cold, bruised and aching. The situation was dire; the best they could hope for was to meet a ship and to replenish some much-needed supplies. They calculated they could survive for a week but after that they would both be lost to the sea!

In calmer seas, having had some food, drink and rest, they felt a little better. Noticing a ship in the far distance, they changed course to intercept it. After tying a blanket to an oar and frantically waving it, someone aboard the ship spotted the small craft. The ship's crew wanted to know where the two men in the rowing boat were from because their unkempt and exceedingly weathered appearance provided no clue. George and Frank were ecstatic when they realised they were talking to fellow Norwegians who were carrying a ship full of Canadian timber to Britain. They accepted an invitation to board the *Cito* where they were given a hearty meal, hot drinks and enjoyed a proper wash! The captain gave them supplies so they might continue their journey. The adventurers offered to pay for these but were told: *'...I'll not take any of your money. It's the least I can do for a fellow Norwegian.'* The two vessels continued on their separate journeys. With replenished supplies, a good meal inside them and having cleaned themselves up, George and Frank felt better than they had for many days. Even better, they had learned that they were only about 1400 kilometres from the Scilly Isles on the edge of Europe.

The Fox and her crew enjoyed calmer conditions for a number of days and were visited by an inquisitive shark and a pod of porpoises. During this period of settled weather, they spotted another ship in the distance which was becalmed in the windless conditions. Hearing voices, members of the crew were surprised to see a small rowing boat beneath them when they peered over the side of their ship.

George and Frank were invited on board and fed a substantial meal. Once again they had happened upon another Norwegian vessel, this one on her way home. Crew members from the *Eugen* listened in amazement as the two rowers relayed their tale. The captain kindly provided them with some kerosene to replace their supply that had been lost during the storm.

As the weather remained stable, George and Frank were able to row long distances. They started to notice more seabirds around them that were known for flying near to land, as well as more ships. George calculated that *The Fox* was on track to reach the Scilly Isles in the far south-west of Britain; knowing they were almost at the end of their journey, they rowed with renewed energy.

They managed to converse with the crew of a Mexican schooner and establish that they were not far from Bishop Rock and its lighthouse. Rowing a small craft in the vicinity of the Scilly Isles was dangerous work considering the number of ships of all sizes that had come to grief upon the islands' rocks.

That night, a beam from the lighthouse pierced through the thick fog. In the light of the new day, the 1st of August 1896, the men rowed towards the black cliffs of the Scillies. Surrounded by huge numbers of crying seabirds, they carefully guided *The Fox* to the shore. They had done it! They had successfully rowed across the North Atlantic Ocean and proved to the many doubters that it could be done. The journey had covered 5262 kilometres and had taken 55 days and 13 hours!

After crossing the North Atlantic Ocean

George and Frank rowed to the main island of St Mary's in the Scilly Isles. As they tied up *The Fox* alongside the pier, a small crowd gathered. After they had explained who they were and where they had come from, the people cheered and gave shouts of praise. Indeed, the onlookers had recently read about the adventurers in the newspapers.

The Fox was greatly admired; she looked in reasonable condition considering the ordeal she had been through which was more than could be said for the crew who looked extremely bedraggled with their grubby oilskins, unkempt hair and beards, weathered faces and hardened leathery hands that displayed numerous sores.

George and Frank walked unsteadily along the road in the settlement of Hugh Town, the muscles in their legs finding it a challenge after so long at sea. They met the United States Consul Agent who certified in their logbook that the pair had completed the journey across the Atlantic. Messages of their success were telegraphed to families and the pair bought fresh food supplies. As they re-joined *The Fox,* photographers arrived to take pictures. After a day of great excitement, the rowers slept well on board their floating home.

George and Frank started the last part of their sea journey to Le Havre by rowing some 400 kilometres to the east along the southern coast of England, overnighting at a couple of locations. As they crossed the English Channel, a small steamer towed them to just outside Le Havre.

At the quay an even larger crowd awaited them, greeting them with smiling faces and kind words in a language they could not understand. They were eventually rescued by a representative from the American Consulate who heartily congratulated them and said how proud the United States was of their incredible achievement. The men were interviewed by a host of reporters and photographers but eventually they were able to visit a nearby public bathhouse before settling down for some serious sleep in a comfortable bed.

After four days exhibiting *The Fox* in Le Havre, George and Frank rowed up the River Seine to Paris. This was an opportunity to start making some money from their adventure, as they had planned, but exhibiting their boat and talking about their journey was somewhat disappointing; although people showed an interest in their adventure, it didn't result in them making much money.

They stayed in the French capital for three weeks before moving on to London where they employed an actor to create a reenactment of their crossing of the Atlantic Ocean. During the performance, entitled *Sons of the Sea,* the actor read and sang songs about their journey as George and Frank pretended to row a boat! The performance was punctuated with flashing lights and crashing cymbals during the storm sequences. It was quite popular and the pair made a significant amount of money, but once they had deducted the expense of the actor, hiring a room to exhibit *The Fox* and their living expenses, the pair made little profit.

After two months George and Frank moved to other cities in Britain to display *The Fox,* but again were disappointed by the response and decided to cancel their visits to other major locations in Europe. Instead, they decided to go straight to Christiana (Oslo) in Norway; surely they would find much more interest in their record-breaking trip in the country where they had been born? If nothing else, it would be an opportunity to reunite with their families.

The adventurers were hailed as heroes in many quarters when they arrived in Norway and enjoyed cheering crowds, speeches, bands playing and a gift of a silver platter at one venue. However, there were others, particularly in some of the Norwegian press, who criticised them for taking on such a risky journey. There was also some hostility because *The Fox* had displayed the American and not the Norwegian flag, which was thought to be unpatriotic!

During a meeting with King Oscar of Norway, the monarch was impressed with their adventure but when it came to presenting the men with a financial reward, gave them only a single 10 Kroner bill each!

Their dream of making a fortune from their journey appeared to be falling apart so George and Frank decided to go back to America. Reporting their return to the United States, one newspaper described their crossing of the Atlantic Ocean as: *The most remarkable event in the way of ocean navigation that ever transpired.*

As promised, the men were presented with medals by Mr Richard Fox, the owner of *The Police Gazette*. George Harbo and Frank Samuelson were the first people to row across any ocean but sadly these exceptionally brave souls did not receive the fame and fortune of which they had dreamed.

Later years

With their adventure over, the two oarsmen had no alternative but to continue with their clamming business. George's family eventually joined him in the United States and by 1908, he and Anine had nine children. By then he had started piloting ships again and, with his earnings, the family moved to a bigger house. In 1908, he received a complete drenching as he boarded a ship whilst piloting, caught pneumonia and died at the age of 44. This came as a shock to his family and, of course, to his close friend Frank.

Frank eventually married a Norwegian woman called Anna. After George's death, Frank his wife and new son returned to Norway where he bought half of his father's farm and started farming again, something he hadn't done for twenty years. When his mother died in 1927, he purchased the other half of the family farm and enjoyed a contented life with his family in rural Norway. He died in 1946 at the age of 76 after a series of illnesses.

Sadly, the story of George and Frank's heroic journey has faded into obscurity. The enormity of their achievement cannot be overstated; using only an open rowing boat of the period, they successfully crossed what is arguably the most challenging route to row across in the Atlantic Ocean. Nobody had ever attempted such a trip before, so they had little idea what challenges they might face. However, with their unwavering determination, incredible physical and mental strength, profound understanding of the sea, navigational skills and reliance on each other, they accomplished the impossible.

Remarkably, the record George and Frank set for two people to row from west to east across the Atlantic Ocean, has never been broken!

George and Frank standing by The Fox

The Fox tied up in Le Havre
(Credit: Long Beach Ice Boat & Yacht Club)

George, Frank and The Fox

The Fox

The story of their journey across the Atlantic Ocean told in the New York Herald, Sunday March 21 1897

Chapter 9

Tom Crean

Tom Crean

Without a tent or any survival equipment and with just a little chocolate and three biscuits, he staggered off into the Antarctic landscape.

Tom Crean was an Irish seaman and adventurer who took part in three Antarctic expeditions at the beginning of the 1900s and made a massive contribution to both Captain Scott's and Ernest Shackleton's expeditions. He was an individual with exceptional physical strength and fortitude who often displayed immense bravery.

Early life

Tom Crean was one of ten siblings born in 1877 into a poor farming family near the village of Annascaul on the Dingle Peninsula in County Kerry. At the age of 12 he left school to work on the family's hill farm.

After arguing with his father when he was 15, he decided to leave home. Tom lied to the authorities, telling them he was 16 in order to enlist in the British Navy. For the next few years he served on a number of different ships sailing to various locations around the world. In 1901, he was fortunate to be in New Zealand at the same time as Captain Scott's ship, *Discovery*, which was on its way to Antarctica to carry out scientific and geographical research. When he learned that the ship was a man short, Tom Crean volunteered to switch vessels and join them on their adventure.

Discovery expedition

After crossing the Southern Ocean in February 1902, Tom and the crew landed at McMurdo Sound off the coast of Antarctica where they constructed a base on the ice at a location they named Hut Point. From there they began their sledging journeys to discover more about this unknown continent.

Tom carried out a variety of daily tasks and learned many new skills in this frozen, inhospitable land. He adapted well to living in polar conditions and was a reliable, popular, good-humoured and physically strong member of the team. Having a tall and strong frame helped him enormously in moving equipment and supplies and, in particular, he was efficient at hauling sledges over the ice when harnessed with other members.

The *Discovery* remained locked in the frozen sea during their stay until February 1904 when it managed to clear itself from the ice and set sail for home. Tom resumed his regular duties in the Royal Navy but, having impressed Captain Scott as a hardworking and reliable individual, Tom joined him on several future ships that he commanded.

Terra Nova expedition

Several years later, Scott asked Tom Crean to join his Terra Nova Expedition to the South Pole. Arriving in January 1911, plans were made for the overland trip to the South Pole. Tom was part of a team whose job it was to take supplies to a food drop some 210 kilometres to the south; this store of food would be used during the journey to the Pole.

When the team returned, they were camping on the ice close to the sea when it began to break up when they were asleep! Suddenly, their sledges and horses were floating on blocks of ice and in danger of being taken out to sea. Tom reacted instinctively to the exceedingly dangerous situation and started leaping from ice floe to ice floe in order to get back onto the main ice sheet. Remarkably, he succeeded and alerted others to help save the lives of those who were adrift.

By November 1911 Captain Scott was ready to make an attempt on the South Pole. The journey would take them about 1390 kilometres across the Great Ice Barrier, up the heavily crevassed Beardmore Glacier onto the final Polar Plateau at 3,000 metres. The aim was to use motor-sledges, ponies and dog teams to carry the mass of supplies required for the journey; man-hauling would be used for the final push to the South Pole once they had reached the plateau. Supporting parties carrying supplies for the expedition would regularly return to base during the trip.

Unfortunately the motor-sledges didn't get very far because they kept breaking down, and the ponies were not suited for polar travel; they continually sank into soft snow because they had not been provided with equine snow shoes. The dogs fared much better when they were carrying loads on sledges, but they were only given less important tasks. Consequently, the expedition members had to haul supplies themselves much earlier than they had planned on their journey south. Inevitably they lost valuable time, used up more food supplies and were greatly fatigued.

Tom Crean, together with William Lashley and Edward Evans, were in the last supporting team to return to base, leaving Captain Scott and four others to continue southwards to the Pole. Tom was devastated at being asked to return just 270 kilometres from their destination as he was considered to be the strongest member of the team. Unfortunately, Edward had become very ill, having suffered from exhaustion, snow-blindness and scurvy.

Their return journey was fraught with problems as they ran out of food and got lost. On one occasion the desperate party slid uncontrollably 600 metres down an icefall! As they desperately held on to their sledge as they slid down the heavily crevassed glacier, they calculated that they had been travelling at around 100kph. It was remarkable that they survived!

As their journey continued, Edward became so ill that Tom and William put him on the sledge to transport him. They continued to man-haul the sledge until they were within 56 kilometres of their base. At that point, Edward collapsed and could go no further.

Their lives were in the balance. What happened next has been described as the greatest single-handed act of bravery in the history of Antarctic exploration. It was decided William would stay with Edward while Tom went to summon help. Without a tent or any survival equipment, and with only a little chocolate and three biscuits, he staggered into the Antarctic landscape. It was an extraordinary act considering he had already walked some 2400 kilometres across Antarctica.

It took Tom 18 hours to cover the distance in the most testing of conditions without any rest but remarkably, totally exhausted, he eventually reached the base. A rescue party was organised and his friends' lives were saved.

Telling the tale after the event, Tom played down his remarkable feat:

So it fell to my lot to do the 30 miles for help, and only a couple of biscuits and a stick of chocolate to do it. Well, sir, I was very weak when I reached the hut.

All through the winter of 1912, the expedition members waited in their hut for Captain Scott and his team to return but it soon became apparent that it was unlikely anyone had survived the harsh Antarctic conditions. In November 1912, at the beginning of the polar summer season, a search party including Tom left the base hoping to locate the missing explorers. They eventually found a tent covered in snow; inside was Scott and other members of the team, frozen to death.

Scott's log informed them that the party had indeed reached the South Pole – but only after Roald Amundson and his team from Norway some 34 days earlier.

The *Nova Terra* left Antarctica early in 1913. Tom was awarded the highest medal for bravery by King George for saving Evans' life.

Endurance *expedition*

Having gained a reputation as an able and gallant polar traveller, Tom Crean joined the *Endurance* expedition led by Ernest Shackleton in May 1914. Their aim was for a party to cross the entire Antarctic continent via the South Pole. Unfortunately, before they could land and disembark in January 1915, their ship became stuck in the ice of the Weddell Sea where they remained locked in drifting ice for many months. Eventually, the huge pressure from the ice crushed and sank the *Endurance* the following November.

The crew had managed to unload food supplies, much of the expedition equipment and three lifeboats before the vessel's demise. They stayed on the ice for five more months until it finally began to break up the following April. The team members were in a severely weakened state, suffering from the intense cold and the trauma of being stranded on drifting sea ice in extreme polar conditions, but they managed to sail and row the three lifeboats to Elephant Island during an extraordinarily difficult five-day journey. Additionally they had to endure seasickness and dysentery. On finding a suitable site on the shore, they gained some respite from their ordeal.

It was clear that most of the crew could not endure further travel, so two boats were upturned for them to await rescue; seals and penguins nearby would supplement their meagre supplies. The third boat was strengthened and prepared for six of the stronger crew members, including Tom, to sail to South Georgia where they knew that whalers were stationed, after which they would return and rescue the remaining crew.

The journey to South Georgia involved crossing some of the wildest seas anywhere on the planet. The party of six left Elephant Island on a 17-day epic journey. Described as probably the most extraordinary feat of seamanship and navigation in history, the already exhausted party of six faced gales, snow squalls and mountainous seas. They rowed, chipped ice from their craft, bailed water and avoided icebergs with very little to eat or drink in continually cold and wet conditions. All through this journey, Tom often sang uplifting Irish songs to raise morale.

They landed on the southern coast of South Georgia – but on the other side of the island to the whaling station at Stromness on the north coast. Completely drained after their exertions at sea, the men desperately tried to work out how to get around the unforgiving waters of the island; sailing wasn't an option as the boat's rudder had broken when they landed. They decided that the three strongest members of the party, Crean, Shackleton and Frank Worsley, would travel the 65 kilometres across the island, an undertaking of huge proportions considering that they had no tent, map or climbing equipment to take them over the mountainous and highly glaciated island. The journey had never been attempted before. They took a carpenter's adze, a length of rope, and they placed screws through their boot soles to act as crampons on the ice.

The journey was dangerous, physically and mentally exhausting with snow, ice and crevasses; they took many wrong directions and had to ascend and descend steep, challenging terrain. Against all the odds, they eventually arrived at the whaling base from where a boat set off to rescue those remaining on the southern coast of the island. However, it took another three months and four rescue attempts to successfully collect the 22 expedition members stranded on Elephant Island. During this period Tom, alongside Shackleton, played a crucial role in persuading the South American authorities to provide resources for the rescue.

Later years

After the *Endurance* expedition, Tom received a third Polar Medal and returned to his regular duties. In 1917 he married Ellen Herlihy in County Kerry. Shackleton asked Tom to join him on another Antarctic expedition but he declined as he was now married and had started a family.

In 1920, Tom left the navy and returned to Ireland, where he opened a pub in the village of Annascaul, which he named The South Pole Inn. He remained a modest man and rarely talked about his adventures in the Antarctic. One of his daughters once commented:

'He put his medals...into a box...and that was that. He was a very humble man.'

Another reason he was secretive about his exploits in the Royal Navy was because it was the height of the Irish independence movement and advertising an involvement with the British probably wouldn't have been advisable. As a consequence, Tom's heroic acts were somewhat suppressed and forgotten, and the accounts written by more famous members of the expeditions have tended to dominate historical records.

Tom adapted well to his new, less-adventurous circumstances and was content with his life in the south-west of Ireland with his wife and three daughters. He passed away at the age of 61.

Tom Crean was an inspirational Irish adventurer who played a significant role during early twentieth-century pioneering expeditions to the Antarctic. His formidable strength, undaunted spirit, bravery and many practical skills made him an ideal person for those early polar journeys.

Expedition ship Endurance just before being crushed by ice in the Wendell Sea, October 1915 (Credit: F Hurley)

Wild seas

Tom and fellow petty officer mending sleeping bags

Scott's South Pole party at 87 degrees south, December 1911, before Crean returned with the last supporting party

Those remaining on Elephant Island waving goodbye to the James Caird

Tom Crean (left) exercising ponies during the winter of 1911

Tom Crean with full polar travelling gear

Chapter 10

Truda Benham

Truda Benham (Credit: Tanzania Horizons Safaris)

At the age of 36, Truda wanted some adventure!

Truda Benham was one of Britain's most prolific travellers of all time. Her journeys involved walking thousands of kilometres in different regions of the world and lasted many months at a time. She climbed 300 major peaks over 3000 metres.

Early life

Gertrude, or 'Truda' as she was known, was born in London in 1867, the youngest of six children to Emily and Frederick Benham. Her father was a master ironmonger who, during summer vacations, explored the European Alps with his family.

It was during these trips that Truda developed a love for adventure and the great outdoors.

She completed a total of 130 ascents in the Alps, which included the Matterhorn and Mont Blanc. By the time she reached her twenties, she had become quite an experienced mountaineer.

During her parents' later years, Truda spent most of her days caring for them. When they passed, she decided to use her small inheritance and her savings to see the world. At the age of 36, Truda wanted some adventure!

Her first adventures

In 1904, Truda travelled to Banff in the heart of the Canadian Rockies where she planned to climb as many mountains as she could. She had the good fortune to meet and climb with the Swiss mountain guides Hans and Christian Kaufman.

Her first foray was Mount Lefroy at 3423 metres. The ascent took place in the rain, which turned to blizzard conditions before the party eventually reached the summit. During the following days she climbed Mount Whyte, Mount Temple and Popes Peak, all around 3000 metres in height.

Truda and her guides moved on to the Valley of the Ten Peaks. During just one day she climbed Mount Fay and Mount Allen, both of which were first ascents, then summited Mount Bowlen a few days later.

Next Truda climbed Mount Stephen, Mount Gordan, Mount Balfour and Mount Collie in the newly designated Yoho National Park, all of which were over 3000 metres. After that she became the first woman to climb the 'Matterhorn-looking' 3618 metre Mount Assiniboine. This challenging peak had only been climbed twice before and took almost a week to ascend. Truda's account of the trip in her diary was very matter of fact, which was very much her nature, with just the words: *Completed the climb of Mount Assiniboine.*

Finally she climbed seven peaks in the Selkirk Mountains, including Mount Rogers (3169 metres) and Swiss Peak (3165 metres) both of which, once again, were first ascents by a woman. Close by in the same massif was an unnamed summit with three sharp pinnacles, which was eventually named 'Truda Peaks' by the authorities *'in recognition of the first lady to ascend Mount Rogers and Swiss Peak – Miss Gertrude Benham of London'.*

At the end of this feast of mountaineering in Canada, Truda set sail for New Zealand by way of Fiji. Arriving in Christchurch early in 1905, she made her way mostly on foot to The Hermitage in the South Island. Staying overnight in farmsteads, she had an enjoyable trek and found the local farmers extremely friendly.

The Hermitage was in the Southern Alps and had become the centre for climbing the surrounding mountains. Truda met local New Zealand guides with whom she completed some lower-level walking and ventured onto a number of glaciers.

She planned to ascend the famed Aoraki (then known as Mount Cook) but there were disagreements about climbing standards that resulted in a lack of summit success during her stay.

After her time in New Zealand, she travelled by ship to Australia, Japan (where she hiked and climbed), India and Egypt before returning to Europe. Truda had completed her first round the world trip, the first of many!

In 1907, she ventured forth once again, this time to Japan then to California before travelling south to Valparaíso in Chile. From there she journeyed across the continent mostly on foot, crossing the Andes and pampas. She once admitted, *'I walk everywhere. I do not care for [horse] riding.'*

After arriving in Buenos Aires in Argentina, she crossed the Atlantic Ocean to Africa and travelled to what is now Kabwe in Zambia. From there she walked 900 kilometres to Mbala at the southern end of Lake Tanganyika. Truda liked to travel alone on these long overland hikes and hire a few local people as porters, guides or cooks when she needed them.

Travelling further north, she climbed in the foothills of the Ruwenzori Mountains before eventually making her way to Nairobi in Kenya, then moving to the town of Voi in the southeast of the country.

Crossing into German East Africa (now Tanzania) at the end of 1909, she walked across open plains to the town of Moshi at the base of Kilimanjaro. Her next project was to ascend the iconic peak. The German commander in the town explained that Africa's highest mountain, *'had never been climbed by any Britisher, man or woman.'* Some days later Truda, together with five porters, two guides and one cook boy, began an ambitious attempt to scale this formidable mountain standing at 5895 metres in height. The mountain had only been climbed for the first time in 1889.

The lower reaches required the party to hack through dense forest before camping just beyond the forest at about 3050 metres. During the next day's hike they came across two human skeletons from a previous expedition. This unnerved the group, particularly the porters who feared for their own lives and refused to go any further.

Truda dismissed such thoughts and continued upwards, reluctantly followed by the remaining two guides and the cook boy. The porters stayed at their previous camp to await their return. After an overnight stay in a cave, Truda carried on alone in her bid to reach the top after the remaining members also decided not to go any further, though they did point out the way to the top. She was now entirely on her own.

At the beginning of the 1900s, glaciers occurred much lower down Kilimanjaro than they do today. Truda's solo climb over snow, ice and rock eventually took her onto the crater rim of the extinct volcano, probably at around 5820 metres and about 75 metres below the actual summit.

My first feeling up there was that of being absolutely on top of the world. The highest point seemed to be some distance to the left.

No other person from Britain, or indeed, any woman in the entire world, had ever climbed so high up Kilimanjaro before. This was quite a milestone in the unfolding history of the mountain. Unfortunately the event wasn't really celebrated, as she was unable to inform many people about her accomplishment.

Truda was often more concerned about her next adventure than advertising her achievements. Indeed, over the next three years the records of her travels are a little vague, though she did visit Kashmir and islands in both the Indian and Pacific Oceans. Where there are gaps in her journals, researchers have searched a number of documents such as passenger lists from ships to complete her story. It is all part of the mystery that surrounds Truda's life!

In 1912, now aged 46, she returned to Africa and took almost a year to complete a 5000 kilometre journey from the Niger delta in Nigeria to Mozambique. Again on foot, Truda travelled through what are now Cameroon, the Central African Republic, Congo, Uganda and Rwanda. Some parts of her journey were through dense forest and swamp, which made progress very slow. She travelled down Lake Tanganyika and Lake Nyasa by steamer and by local canoe, and climbed Mount Nyiragongo and Mount Mularje, both over 3000 metres in height.

Along the way, Truda had a close encounter with four lions whilst she was camping. She explained:

I have been quite close to lions and leopards in the bush but they have never harmed me...I always go unharmed and I think wild animals...know by instinct that I have no desire to kill.

The epic overland journey ended at Chinde on the Indian Ocean coast in Mozambique. As on her other long journeys, Truda spent some of her spare time sketching, painting, collecting flowers and taking photographs, as well as repairing or making her own clothes. She also embroidered and knitted items which she later exchanged for local artefacts along the way.

To stay healthy, Truda believed in only eating local food, taking exercise and always sleeping under a mosquito net in tropical regions. On one occasion in India when she slept under a torn net, she came down with malaria. One other key element to her remaining healthy was '*taking plenty of liquid, mainly tea or hot water, and salt with one's food*'.

From Mozambique she sailed to Zanzibar and the Seychelles before disembarking at Bombay, from where she made her way to Shimla in the Himalayan mountains. She spent an entire summer walking many hundreds of kilometres to Srinagar, crossing the 4000 metre Rotang Pass along the way. Most of this trip was over 3,000 metres in height. This involved many days of challenging travel in rugged terrain and freezing conditions; she had to make her way beside one treacherous Himalayan river surrounded by rock falls and avalanche debris and cross a raging torrent by rope bridge.

Truda arrived back in Britain in the spring of 1916 at the height of World War One.

Her later adventures

Having spent the next two years in Britain, as soon as the fighting stopped Truda went to India. For more than six months she trekked from Naini Tal to Leh in northern India, crossing snow-covered passes, following river valleys and being completely surrounded by high mountains. It was a testing 1300 kilometre journey.

Another trip around the world, her fifth, took place during the following three years although there are some gaps in her itinerary. In 1920, she was again in India and spent two months in the Seychelles before sailing to Mombasa in Kenya and making her way to the north of the country. Once there, she climbed Mount Elgon on two separate occasions to collect plant specimens for the Natural History Museum in London. This vast volcanic mountain, its highest point at 4321 metres, straddles Kenya and Uganda. The peak possessed a huge variety of flora for Truda to observe and collect.

After going to southern Africa by ship, she spent weeks hiking in the Drackensberg Mountains and Zululand before sailing to Western Australia and returning to Britain.

Between 1923 and 1925, Truda spent time in India and Tibet. She applied to the British colonial authorities to enter Tibet but was informed that permission could only be granted via Sikkim. This didn't suit her plans, so she embarked on a trek through northern Indian valleys close to Mount Kamet and Nanda Devi.

It was the monsoon season and Truda experienced many challenges: on one occasion her tent collapsed after hours of heavy snowfall. Eventually, she crossed into Tibet by way of Sikkim just as the authorities had originally suggested, then completed an eight-week long trek.

After a brief return to Britain, she was soon on her sixth world tour, though once again she recorded few details. She visited East Africa, the Middle East and the Far East, before sailing across the Pacific to the Americas.

In 1929, Truda was back in the Himalaya, seeking permission to cross the border into Tibet again. Her somewhat awkward relationship with the colonial authorities resulted in them compiling a secret dossier suggesting that Gertrude Benham was, *'a bad type of British traveller to be allowed to enter Tibet'.*

In 1931, at the age of 64, Truda spent almost a year camping in remote locations or living in villages in the Himalaya; there is nothing recorded to say that she didn't succeed in secretly entering Tibet at some point.

After her Himalayan adventure, Truda completed her seventh journey around the planet by stopping at Hong Kong, California, Peru and Chile.

Her phenomenal appetite for travel never abated. In an interview on her return, she stated she had *'visited every part of the British Empire, except Tristan da Cunha and a few other small islands'.* In 1935, she embarked on what was intended to be her eighth and final trip around the world. She visited the New Hebrides (Vanuatu), New Zealand, India and South Africa then travelled overland to the East African coast, where she boarded a ship, destination unknown.

At the age of 71, somewhere off the coast of East Africa, Truda died and was buried at sea. It was the end of a remarkable life of an adventurer who wanted to experience the splendour of the entire world. As Truda once admitted:

I am a lone wanderer...there is nothing to prevent me enjoying...the spirit of wanderlust that has entered my soul...there is so much to see and admire in the world.

For 35 years she had journeyed around the globe. She defied the expectations set for women of the time: home making, raising a family and supporting a patriarchal society. Her extraordinary trips remained largely unknown for a long time but the incredible achievements of this exceptional world traveller's life have slowly been revealed in more recent times.

Kilimanjaro crater in 1904 (Credit: Carl Uhlig)

The main square in the town of Leh in northern India, early 1900s

Mount Assiniboine, Canadian Rockies

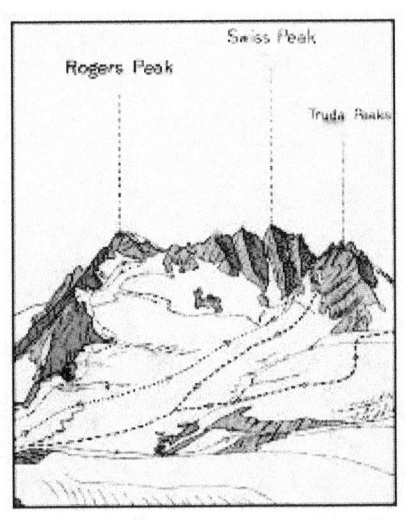

The Selkirk Mountains Roger's Peak and Swiss Peak, first ascents by a woman. 'Truda Peaks' named in her honour.

Truda camping in Nyasaland (Malawi) in 1913 (Credit: Tanzania Horizons Safaris)

Chapter 11

Joshua Slocum

Joshua Slocum

He had become the first person to sail alone around the world.

Between 1895 and 1898, Joshua Slocum became the first person to sail single-handedly around the world. The Canadian-American completed the circumnavigation in an ageing vessel named *Spray,* which he had rebuilt himself.

Early life

Joshua was born in 1844 in Mount Hanley, Nova Scotia, Canada. He was the fifth of eleven children born into a farming family. After struggling to make a living, the family moved to Brier Island, Nova Scotia, where his mother, Sarah, had grown up as the daughter of the lighthouse keeper. His father, John, opened a tanning and boot-making shop for the local fishermen.

At the age of ten Joshua was taken out of school to help his father in the shop. Softening cowhide with its overpowering odour for ten hours every day was hard work. Throughout this period, Joshua longed to be out with his friends patching up boats and trying his hand at sailing and rowing, and watching seagoing vessels pass by.

He dreamed continually of a life on the ocean. On one occasion, Joshua's father caught him secretly making a model ship in the shop. A strict disciplinarian, his father smashed the carefully constructed model into pieces. After the incident, Joshua wanted to free himself from his home life and run away to sea.

His first attempt to escape at fourteen ended in failure. He signed up as a cabin boy on a fishing schooner, but when he returned home he received a good thrashing from his father. After his mother died two years later, Joshua successfully ran away and signed up on a vessel carrying Canadian timber to Dublin.

It was a hard introduction: novice sailors were expected to work long hours in very challenging conditions. After this first voyage, Joshua sailed to Liverpool and embarked on a British ship bound for China.

After spending the next two years aboard several ships travelling the world, Joshua gradually gained experience. He wanted to learn as much as he could, and was particularly keen to master the art of navigation. He learned to take sightings by using a sextant to calculate a ship's position and in due course became a master navigator.

By the time he was eighteen, Joshua was a fully qualified second mate. He moved to the west coast of the United States, became an American citizen and started fishing for salmon along the Columbia River. Together with a friend he designed and built a fishing boat, a project he enjoyed very much. He also became involved with sea otter hunting and traded furs along the north-west coast of the United States.

Captain of the high seas

Joshua's real ambition was to command his own ship. This came to fruition when he was just twenty-five years of age and became captain of a schooner named *Montana* carrying food supplies along the California coast.

Not long after that, Joshua was given the command of a bigger vessel transporting items further afield, which eventually took him to Sydney, Australia. Whilst there, Joshua had a whirlwind romance with Virginia, a young lady originally from the USA; in a matter of weeks they were married and sailed together when he left Sydney.

So began their married life on board ship, since Virginia preferred to sail with her husband rather than stay in port. During the following years, Joshua continued to sail to various parts of the world delivering cargo. The couple had seven children in total, all born either at sea or in foreign ports. Virginia taught them to read and write and even persuaded her husband to bolt an upright piano to the deck so they could learn to play music. Sadly, three of the children died; only three boys and one daughter survived.

Whilst sailing the ship *Washington* close to the Alaskan coastline, the vessel began breaking up. Using open boats, and at considerable risk to himself, Joshua saved his family, the crew and much of the cargo. Around this time, he also became a temporary correspondent for the *San Francisco Bee* newspaper and realised his ambition of becoming a writer.

In 1881, at the age of 37, he took command of his biggest ship to date, the three-masted, three-decked, *Northern Light*. He was very proud of his new vessel, describing it as the finest American sailing ship afloat. It not only had a greater capacity for carrying cargo but also gave the Slocums more space as a family.

His adventurous and resourceful wife was in many ways essential to the success of their travelling partnership. Virginia's quick thinking was well illustrated when a mutiny took place aboard the *Northern Light*. After one sailor had been stabbed, Virginia, brandishing a revolver in each hand, brought the situation under control. Later there was another mutiny aboard the same ship where the ringleader was eventually incarcerated. Unfortunately Joshua was later fined for mishandling the affair; the event dented his reputation as a captain and he was forced to give up *Northern Light* for a much smaller vessel.

Living a hard life at sea and raising a large family eventually took its toll on Virginia's health and she died of heart failure just before her 35th birthday. This devastated Joshua; one of his sons described his father like *'a ship with a broken rudder'*.

Within two years, Joshua had married his cousin, Hettie, with whom he continued a life at sea. During Hettie's inaugural trip as the captain's wife upon his new ship *Aquidneck,* there was a series of devastating events including a hurricane, an outbreak of cholera onboard and, later on, smallpox which killed three crew members. Joshua faced another mutiny, during which he shot dead one of the crew; the Brazilian authorities arrested him but he was eventually released after an investigation.

In 1887, the *Aquidneck* ran aground after crashing into a sandbar off the coast of Brazil and Joshua and his family were stranded! Ever the resourceful mariner, he salvaged enough material from the wreckage to build a large canoe-like vessel. The craft was named *Liberdade,* the Portuguese word for 'freedom', and launched on the day that slavery was abolished in Brazil. Although they were subject to extremely stormy conditions during which the sails were completely ruined, they accomplished the voyage of almost 9,000 kilometres in fifty-five days.

Arriving back in the United States, Hettie and the children went to stay with relatives. Unlike Virginia, his second wife hadn't taken to a life aboard ship with all of its associated adventures! When she was asked if she would ever go to sea again, she politely replied: *'Oh, I hope not. I haven't been home for three years, and this was my wedding voyage.'*

Joshua wrote about their experiences in a book entitled *Voyage of the Liberdade*. After it was finished, he didn't know what to do with his life. He had lost his ship, his career, his reputation, his family – and he was penniless.

The first solo circumnavigation

One day in 1892, as Joshua was strolling along Boston's waterfront, he fell into conversation with a retired whaling captain. To his surprise, the man offered Joshua a ship that had been hauled up in his garden for seven years. Unfortunately, the 11 by 4 metre vessel, a century-old oyster sloop named *Spray*, needed a complete overhaul.

Joshua accepted the offer and immediately set to work, happy to have a renewed purpose to his life. The roughly constructed vessel needed most parts replacing and updating to make it seaworthy. To help pay for these refurbishments, he took a temporary job delivering an iron gunboat named *Destroyer* to Brazil; however, the ship was sunk during the voyage.

It was an epic journey, after which Joshua decided to write a second book, *Voyage of the Destroyer from New York to Brazil*. After it was published, he was challenged to a duel! Evidently somebody attached to the military hadn't liked certain comments he had made in his book!

Spray was eventually rebuilt, providing fifty-one-year-old Joshua with a refurbished vessel. He had been at sea for most of his life, sailed around the world five times and accumulated a vast understanding of sea conditions, the weather and navigation

– but he was at a loss as to what to do with his new boat. Finally he hit upon the idea of sailing alone around the world!

Once the decision was made, Joshua spent his time making *Spray* ready for the journey and storing enough food supplies to last for weeks until they could be replenished. He took a library of books on board and some firearms to guard himself against attack. On April 24, 1895, *Spray* and her captain left the harbour in Boston. Joshua wrote:

A thrilling pulse beat high in me...I felt there could be no turning back, and that I was engaged in an adventure the meaning of which I thoroughly understood...Waves dancing joyously across Massachusetts Bay...The day was perfect, the sunlight clear and strong...Every particle of water thrown into the air became a gem...

Joshua's first port of call was his childhood home, Brier Island in Nova Scotia. After that, he headed straight into the North Atlantic to the Azores and on to Gibraltar. He had intended to sail west to east, across the Mediterranean Sea and through the Suez Canal but, after discussions with several people in the port, he learned that this route was fraught with danger. At that time the Mediterranean was awash with pirate ships intent on plundering vessels, especially smaller craft.

As a consequence, Joshua made fresh plans. He decided to travel east to west around the globe and prepared to sail across the Atlantic again. After he left Gibraltar and was nearing the coast of Morocco, a local *felucca* sailing boat full of Moorish pirates started following *Spray*. As soon as it changed direction, the felucca did the same. With the pirates gaining ground, Joshua readied his guns; he was relieved when their craft was unable to sail through heavier waves further on in the chase.

Continuing across the Atlantic, *Spray* sailed by the Canary Islands and the Cape Verde Islands before being becalmed in the mid-Atlantic doldrums. Forty days after leaving Gibraltar, *Spray* anchored in Pernambuco Harbour, Brazil, before continuing to Rio de Janeiro.

Joshua made repairs to the craft before continuing south along the South American coast. Unfortunately, when sailing a little too close to land, the vessel was beached off the Uruguayan coast. In his lightweight boat, or dory, Joshua rowed away from *Spray*. Using his anchor and rope, he performed a manoeuvre to try and break free from the sand bank. He tried this several times, at one point, managing to upturn his dory and becoming completely submerged in the water. This could have been catastrophic because, as he said afterwards, *'I suddenly remembered that I could not swim!'*

Local villagers came to his rescue and *Spray* was eventually freed. Joshua sailed to nearby Montevideo where the damage to the ship and its dory was repaired. After visiting Buenos Aires, he sailed south and eventually reached the entrance to the Strait of Magellan. He was about to enter one of the most difficult and dangerous stretches of water in the world.

His journey began with more than thirty hours of gales, fierce rain squalls, high waves, strong tides and currents. *Spray* made its way to the Chilean port of Punta Arenas, part way along the strait, where Joshua was warned about unruly local bandits on the next leg of his journey; led by a character called Black Pedro, they were in the habit of raiding passing ships.

He continued carefully in tempestuous weather and sea conditions before dropping anchor each night. It wasn't long before he realised he was being pursued by a number of canoes. Joshua was keen to show his pursuers he was not alone so he surreptitiously changed his outer clothing and rapidly constructed a scarecrow to create the illusion of more than one person onboard. Reaching for his guns, he fired at his pursuers.

He continued through the strait in yet more wild weather. As a precaution when he anchored overnight, he took to scattering carpet tacks across the deck. This paid off because one night he was woken abruptly by shrieks of pain as his pursuers tried to board *Spray* and saw men leaping into canoes.

Joshua encountered Black Pedro and his gang on other occasions before leaving those problematic waters. After spending more than two months in the Straits of Magellan, battling through horrendous conditions, he finally sailed into the Pacific Ocean. In so doing, he had become the first person in history to sail solo through the 570 kilometre narrow sea link between the Atlantic and Pacific Oceans.

Joshua made for the Juan Fernández Island off the coast of Chile where he stayed for a number of days. It was a unique, isolated place:

...a lovely spot. The hills are wooded, the valleys fertile, and pouring down through many ravines are streams of pure water.

With a population of only 45 souls, Joshua took great delight in being shown around this idyllic spot describing his visit as quite possibly...*the pleasantest on my whole voyage.*

Catching the trade winds, he sailed west past the Marquesas Islands and carried on until he reached Samoa. This leg of his trip necessitated sailing for seventy-two days with nothing but the ocean and its creatures – and his many books – for companions.

Dropping anchor in Apia, Samoa, Joshua was greeted by local inhabitants including Fanny Stevenson, the widow of the author, Robert Louis Stevenson, who lived there. After visiting the islands and enjoying the local customs and ceremonies, it was again time to up anchor.

Sailing north of Fiji, *Spray* eventually reached Newcastle in Australia after forty-two days of sailing and riding out many storms.

Joshua stayed in Australia for a number of months, where he made repairs to his ship. Visiting Tasmania, Melbourne and

Sydney, he gave public lectures about his journey and invited people onboard *Spray*; charging for their visit helped pay for expenses he would incur during the remaining part of his circumnavigation.

Joshua eventually sailed up the eastern coast of Australia to Thursday Island in the Torres Strait in the far north. From there, he sailed westward for twenty-three days across the Indian Ocean to the Cocos Islands. *Spray*'s cleverly devised self-steering system meant he could sail confidently for days at a time on a given course. During such periods, weather permitting, he could again take to his books and relax.

From the Cocos Islands he visited Rodriguez Island before continuing to Mauritius, where he decided to stay for a while. Next he sailed *Spray* through gales and electrical storms to Durban in South Africa. After sailing around the Cape of Good Hope in rough seas, he eventually cast anchor in Cape Town. *Spray* was placed in dry dock for three months while Joshua visited parts of the country by train, delivering lectures and attending receptions. His journey around the world was beginning to create an interest.

In March 1898, he set off across the Atlantic, travelling north-west towards St Helena, where he was the guest of the governor of the island. On leaving, Joshua was presented with a goat. The extra passenger turned out to be somewhat of a liability; the creature's appetite was such that it ate Joshua's straw hat, the rope tethering it and, most serious of all, consumed the vessel's sea charts for the West Indies! At his next destination, Ascension Island, an exasperated Joshua decided to leave his unruly gift to fend for itself.

After crossing the equator, he sailed north-west to the West Indies. No longer having any sea charts, he had to rely on his memory to identify areas that were dangerous. He stopped at the islands of Grenada and Dominica before sailing towards the United States.

During this final part of his journey, Joshua experienced a range of conditions including gales, electrical storms and a tornado, as well as being becalmed. Finally, on July 3rd, 1898, *Spray* sailed into Fairhaven Harbour, Massachusetts in the United States. He had become the first person to sail alone around the world, a route of 74,000 kilometres that had taken him three years and two months.

Later life

There was a subdued response to Joshua's extraordinary journey in America. At the time, the nation was more concerned about recent political events, most notably the declaration of war between the United States and Spain two weeks earlier. However, news of Joshua's arrival gradually spread.

Unfortunately, there were many who were sceptical about whether he had actually completed the journey. Some said that it was impossible to sail alone in such a small craft, around the entire globe but Joshua was pleased to prove the doubters wrong by producing signed confirmation from each port he had visited. In time, his amazing achievement was recognised.

Joshua wrote a book about his circumnavigation, with *Century Magazine* publishing sections of his story in installments. When *Sailing Alone Around The World* was eventually finished it received positive reviews and became an international best seller. *The Nautical Gazette* commented:

There is no question as to his name being handed down to posterity as one of the most intrepid of navigators.

Joshua made enough money from his book and lectures about his trip to make a few changes to his life. Together with his estranged wife, Hettie, he bought a house and a plot of land in Martha's Vineyard, Massachusetts. For the previous sixteen years, the couple had been apart and Hettie had been forced to live with various relatives.

Joshua made an effort to grow vegetables and fruit, as well as making alterations to his new home, but after a year and a half he found it difficult to adapt to a life ashore. Sometimes he slipped away and stayed on board *Spray,* which was moored nearby.

Wanting to escape back to a life at sea, Joshua started sailing to north-eastern American ports during the summertime to give lectures and sell his books. During the winter months, he sailed south to the Caribbean Islands where he collected shells and coral to sell after he returned home. Eventually he and Hettie resorted to living separate lives once again.

Many people observed that the captain was becoming both physically and mentally run down; *Spray* was also in need of some care, not having been overhauled in a long time. Despite this Joshua, at the age of 65, announced that he was going to have one more great adventure. His plan was to sail *Spray* to Venezuela then explore the Orinoco River, the Rio Negro and the Amazon.

In November 1909, he sailed out of Vineyard Haven into the open sea. Unfortunately, neither he nor *Spray* were ever seen again! What exactly happened to Joshua and his ship is one of the sea's mysteries. There was speculation that the journey was too much for the ship, that for some reason it couldn't handle the conditions, and it broke up and sank. Another theory was that *Spray* was hit by a much bigger steamer ship, perhaps during the night when it couldn't be seen. Eventually the famous sea captain was declared dead, missing at sea.

It was the end of a man whose entire being was entwined with sailing and the sea. His incredible single-handed circumnavigation has written Captain Joshua Slocum into marine history.

The Spray

Tragedy off the coast of Uruguay! 'I suddenly remembered that I could not swim!' (Credit: Project Gutenberg)

Greetings from Samoans

Reading aboard Spray

Chapter 12

Elizabeth Le Blond

Elizabeth Le Blond

The rocks were big and firm. We were able to thrust fingers and toes into good, honest holds, and towards the end we met the chimney which was bliss to go up.

Elizabeth Le Blond achieved an incredible catalogue of mountaineering feats both in the Alps and in Arctic Norway. As well as her climbing achievements, she was also a pioneer in the fields of both mountain photography and moviemaking.

Early years

Elizabeth was born in 1860 and brought up in the town of Greystones, in the south-east of Ireland. Her aristocratic family owned extensive swathes of land in the counties of Wicklow,

Dublin and Meath. After the death of her father, she inherited the family estate at the age of eleven. Elizabeth enjoyed a happy childhood and took a keen interest in everything around her, though she disliked formal school lessons.

When she was nineteen she married Colonel Frederick Burnaby, aged 38, who was a soldier, adventurer and writer. In 1880, the couple had a son, Harry, but soon after this they started living apart most of the time. After developing lung problems, Elizabeth decided to travel in search of a climate that might improve her health whilst Frederick returned to his life in the army.

The Alps

Elizabeth's travels took her to the Alps, a move that subsequently changed her life. She wrote:

In the summer of 1881 I came to Chamonix for the first time. I arrived there in bad health. As for mountaineering, I knew nothing of it...

After spending some time in the pure mountain air, she appeared to be in much better physical condition and began to appreciate her surroundings:

I saw for the first time those glacier-clad Alpine ranges which were to mean so much to me for the rest of my life.

Unable to resist the lure of the Alps, one of her first outings was to scramble two-thirds of the way up Mont Blanc, the highest of all the Alpine peaks. The following summer, she climbed to the very top not once but on two separate occasions. She also ascended a number of other significant peaks in the area.

So began Elizabeth's love of mountaineering. For the next twenty years, climbing with guides, she made more than 100 ascents throughout the Alps. As she established herself as a competent mountaineer, she became renowned for her courage, physical strength, stamina and good judgement. Her ascents included the Matterhorn, Grandes Jorasses, Dent du Géant and the Zinalrothorn – the latter she succeeded in climbing twice in one day! In keeping with the sensitivities of the period, Elizabeth started each climb wearing a dress, but, once out of sight, changed into more practical riding breeches for the ascent.

As her mountaineering experience increased, she made more challenging winter ascents of Alpine passes and peaks. She often met with extreme conditions, including blizzards, very cold temperatures, strong winds, deep snow and poor visibility. Given the rudimentary nature of her climbing attire, this sometimes led to serious consequences; on more than one occasion, she had brushes with frostbite.

She made the first winter traverse of Piz Palü, together with the first winter ascents of several high passes in the Chamonix area. Such daring climbs included a winter attempt on the Monte Rosa before being turned back by poor weather close to the summit. She also completed the first winter ascent of the Aiguille du Midi:

Chamonix lay at our feet, and a puff of smoke followed later by a "boom" announced that the good people below had seen our arrival, and were firing a cannon in our honour.

Elizabeth had proved that she was a perfectly capable climber in a variety of mountaineering situations in all seasons of the year.

Norway

Later in her climbing career, she ventured into Arctic Norway to climb in the Lyngen Alps. With her Alpine guide friend, Joseph Imboden, and his son, Emil, she spent six summers ascending a total of 33 mountains, 27 of which were first ascents.

At the time most of these peaks hadn't been climbed before; indeed, many had not even been named! Elizabeth and her party named the mountains according to the nearby features and character of the mountain, which they translated into Norwegian.

> ...these magnificent mountains...we marvelled at their grandeur and extent.

Travelling in these northern mountains wasn't always easy, given their remote location. Any ascent invariably involved a journey by boat along fjords then walking over difficult terrain before they could start climbing. These climbers were pioneering new routes up virgin mountains; they were very much on their own in an unfamiliar landscape and exposed to constantly changing weather conditions. However, the mountaineering was extremely gratifying, as Elizabeth wrote after one of her successes:

> ...we had the very best climb I enjoyed that summer. The rocks were big and firm. We were able to thrust fingers and toes into good, honest holds, and towards the end we met the chimney which was bliss to go up.

If the weather held, she enjoyed a view of mile after mile of fjords and snow-crowned mountains.

Photography and film making

As well as becoming a competent mountaineer, Elizabeth was one of the first mountain photographers. From the beginning of her climbing career she always carried a camera to capture the inspirational scenery that had never been documented close up. This was during the very early years of photography when the equipment was unwieldy and cumbersome. Wrestling with a camera and setting it up ready for a picture during windy, snowy, freezing and generally bad physical conditions wasn't always straightforward; trying to adjust screws with frozen hands, and with the focusing cloth continually blowing away, taking mountain photographs could be difficult. As time moved on Elizabeth was able to use some of the lighter equipment that was being manufactured and her job became a little easier.

Her love of mountain photography was illustrated when she wrote:

Surely a mountain freshly covered with a robe of pure, white snow is as unsullied a thing of beauty as we can ever gaze on...To me snow-texture is an extraordinary beautiful thing...I am always urging others to open their eyes as wide as possible to the endless variety of its lights and shadows.

She not only took photographs during her climbs but also developed and printed them. During her climbing career, she took thousands of photographs of which about 400 have been used in publications. She gave away some of these pictures as gifts and turned others into magic lantern slides to use during her lectures. To help others who wanted to take snow photographs, Elizabeth printed a manual entitled *Hints on Snow Photography* in 1895.

As the technology improved, she started using the first movie-cameras of the time and became the world's first mountain filmmaker. Amongst her films are short movies about Alpine winter sports in the Engadine valley of Switzerland, including bobsleigh, ice hockey, tobogganing and figure skating. In her collection of photographs and short films are images of the famous Cresta Run, in which Elizabeth became involved whilst living in St Moritz.

Later years

Adding to her list of achievements, she was the first woman to pass the prestigious men's ice-skating test of the St Moritz Skating Association. As well as mountain-related activities, she completed cycle tours that included cycling from the Alps across France and back to Britain.

Elizabeth's marriage to Frederick Burnaby ended in 1885 after he was killed in battle in Sudan. In 1886 she married Dr John Main, a mathematician. Sadly, this marriage also ended after he fell ill and died in 1892 while he was visiting the United States. In 1900, she married for a third time to Aubrey Le Blond.

Elizabeth was key in creating the British Ladies' Alpine Club in 1907 since women were not allowed to be members of the already established Alpine Club. She was its first president and spent considerable time providing information and encouragement to women climbers. She also wrote about her experiences in the mountains and published a total of eight books.

Elizabeth gradually stopped active climbing. In 1912, she and Aubrey took a world tour during which they visited North Africa, Eastern Asia and Russia. At the outbreak of World War One, she travelled to Dieppe to work as a volunteer nurse and spent time raising funds for the elite French Mountain Infantry Unit. By 1916, she had become the director of fundraising for the wartime British Ambulance Committee.

For such dedicated work, Elizabeth was awarded the French Cross of the Légion d'Honneur in 1933. After a short illness, she died in 1934 at the age of 74. Her life was truly inspirational.

Elizabeth's photography – descent from Piz Bermina in Switzerland

A crevasse on the Sella Pass, Italy

In the Alps

Toboggan preparation at the top of the Cresta Run, St. Moritz, Switzerland

Walking in the Alps

Climbing in the Alps

Elizabeth's book 'Hints on Snow Photography'. She sometimes published under the name Mrs Main

Elizabeth's photography - A climber on the Morteratsch Glacier, Switzerland

Elizabeth's photography: The Cresta Run

Chapter 13

Norman Collie

Norman Collie

A new world was spread at our feet: to the westward stretched a vast icefield probably never before seen by the human eye.

Norman Collie was a mountaineer, explorer and one of the country's leading scientists. At the beginning of the last century he made many first ascents and established a host of new climbing routes in Scotland, the Alps, Norway and the Canadian Rockies. In 1895, he took part in one of the first attempts to climb an 8000 metre high peak in the Himalaya.

Earlier life

Norman was born in 1859 in Alderley Edge in Cheshire, into a family whose wealth had come from the cotton trade. After his schooling he studied chemistry at university and eventually received a PhD in the subject. He started his professional life by teaching in a school and then worked in the chemistry department at University College, London.

For pleasure he went on fishing trips to Scotland, one of which took him to the Isle of Skye in 1886. As the conditions for fishing were poor, Norman found himself wandering around the island's Cuillin Hills. So began his great love for the mountains. He described a land:

> ...where the wild west winds sweep straight from the ocean - a lonely land, where one can wander far from the haunts of men, following the streams as they flow seaward through the quiet valleys.

During his many visits to the island he met John Mackenzie, the country's first professional mountain guide. Together they completed a great number of pioneering climbs in the Cuillins, including the first ascent of the unique rock features Sron na Ciche (the Cioch), Am Basteir (the Basteir Tooth) and many others. By 1888, Norman had climbed all the peaks on Skye and a great friendship had evolved between the two men which lasted for the rest of their lives.

Norman was instrumental in developing more detailed maps of the Cuillin Mountains and in recognition of his pioneering work on the Isle of Skye, one of the peaks was named after him: 'Sgùrr Thormaid' is Gaelic for 'Norman's Peak'.

He began visiting other upland areas of Britain at a time when a few adventurous characters were beginning to explore more challenging ascents within the hills. He visited the Lake District where his first ascents included rock-climbing routes on several peaks such as Great Gable, Buckbarrow and Scafell. He climbed these with a band of friends who were also forging new ways up mountains.

In addition, Norman completed new routes on the Scottish mainland; he made several first ascents in Glencoe, including on the Buachaille Etive Mor and Bidean nam Bian. On Ben Nevis he completed the first winter ascents of both Castle Ridge and Tower Ridge. Of the latter, he said that it was the best climb he had ever completed in Scotland.

To higher mountains

Between 1892 and 1894, Norman visited the Alps and climbed with friends, including Alfred Mummery, Geoffrey Hastings and Cecil Slingsby. These climbers advocated the relatively new concept of ascending mountains without employing local guides. Ever since mountaineering had begun in the Alps, it had been the tradition for visiting climbers to hire the services of mountain guides from centres such as Chamonix or Zermatt. However, some foreign visitors were in the mood for change. They were convinced that without guides climbers would have to make their own decisions, overcome the challenges that they faced and thus have a more all-round mountain experience.

Norman and his friends climbed a number of new routes including a traverse of the Aiguille de Grépon and new climbs on the Dent du Requin, the Aiguille du Plan and the Grand Combin.

In 1895, Norman, Mummery and Hastings went to the Himalaya in order to climb the 8126 metre Nanga Parbat. This was the first time in history that an 8000 metre peak had ever been attempted; these were the early days of Himalayan exploration when only a few teams had successfully scaled any of the mountains, let alone one of the highest.

Norman wrote:

...it was the satisfaction of going where others have feared to tread...the delight of seeing mighty glaciers and superb snow-clad peaks never gazed upon before by human eyes.

Scaling one of the highest peaks on the planet was exceedingly ambitious; they were very much stepping into the unknown.

After a period of initial exploration of the Nanga Parbat area, the climbers ventured ever higher and decided to climb nearby Diamirai Peak. This was an opportunity to climb to higher altitudes before they attempted their intended peak; with a height of 5570 metres, they didn't know what the ascent would be like and how their bodies would function at such altitude.

Norman, together with Mummery, a Gurkha, Ragobir Singh, and a local tribesman, Lor Khan, successfully ascended this previously unclimbed peak. After that they started their grand push to climb the considerably higher Nanga Parbat. A number of their attempts were unsuccessful due to poor weather conditions, challenging climbing, the effects of altitude, and illness.

On their final attempt Mummery, Ragobir and a fellow Gurkha, Goman Singh, failed to return; Norman had been ill so he had remained behind. After an extensive search lasting many days in different locations, it was concluded that the party had been swept away by an avalanche from the Rakhiot Face of Nanga Parbat. Norman was deeply saddened by their deaths.

The Canadian Rockies

In 1897, Norman went to climb and explore in the Canadian Rockies, a vast and largely unexplored mountainous expanse. He was immediately impressed with this land of wild, beautiful and untouched terrain. His intention was to climb with mountaineers from both sides of the Atlantic.

To journey within this vast, forested land required hiring an 'outfit' of skilled locals with horses and provisions to transport them and overcome any logistical challenges they encountered . Crossing flooded rivers where strong currents threatened to sweep away horses, their riders and provisions was always problematic; in addition, they would have to hack trails through densely wooded areas, fallen trees and thick underbrush often rife with mosquitoes, which required a great deal of physical toil and discomfort.

Norman took part in a total of six expeditions to the Canadian Rockies between 1897 and 1911, recording 21 first ascents and naming at least 30 peaks. Amongst these were Mount Lefroy (3423 metres), Mount Victoria (3464 metres), Diadem Peak (3371 metres), Mount Forbes (3612 metres) and Neptuak Mountain (3241 metres). Any problems in ascending these unclimbed mountains were worked out as they were explored. This was adventuring in the extreme.

An example of mountaineering danger in such an untouched land occurred in 1897. Norman's party was crossing a glacier after successfully ascending a new peak, Mount Gordon, at 3161 metres. Suddenly one of their members, Charles Thompson, fell head first into a deep crevasse!

Norman decided he would be lowered by rope down the hole to rescue his fellow climber. After descending about 50 metres by rope, he still could not reach Thompson who, although unhurt, was completely wedged upside down between ice. It took an immense effort for Norman to tie another rope around his friend's arm. The situation was dire, but remarkably both climbers were eventually extracted unharmed from the crevasse.

In 1898 Norman, with Hugh Stutfield and Hermann Woolley, climbed the 3491 metre Mount Athabasca, one of the most enjoyable climbs he made in the Rockies. From the summit they were privileged to be amongst the first to see the vast Columbia Icefield, the most extensive glacial area in the Canadian Rockies:

The view that lay before us in the evening light was one that does not often fall to the lot of modern mountaineers. A new world was spread at our feet: to the westward stretched a vast ice-field probably never before seen by the human eye, and surrounded by entirely unknown, unnamed and unclimbed peaks.

These were truly unique pioneering times!

Later years

Having been persuaded by fellow climbers, Norman went to the Lofoten Islands in the far north of Norway during the summers of 1901, 1903 and 1904. With its position north of the Arctic Circle, it was possible to climb for most of the day in this land of almost perpetual light.

Norman was impressed by the rugged mountains that rose abruptly from the fjords and had striking, glacially sculpted features. As in the Rockies, most of these peaks were unclimbed even though none were more than 1200 metres in height.

Exploring the islands was often a challenge: journeying by boat could be problematic, and once ashore he had to negotiate difficult terrain. There was often heavy rain to contend with, together with plagues of mosquitoes. However, he enjoyed great days of exploration and achieved numerous climbing successes. During his three visits to the Lofoten Islands, Norman and his companions climbed 16 new summits including Higraftind (1161m), Geitgaljartind (1083 m), Hermandalstind (1033 metres) and Rulten (1062m).

Over the years Norman had become one of the leading scientists in the country and eventually became a professor of organic chemistry at University College London in 1896. Amongst his many scientific achievements was the development of the neon lamp and pioneering the use of X-ray photography in medicine.

A lifelong bachelor, he had a number of additional interests. He was an expert on Chinese and Japanese artwork and possessed a considerable personal collection. He was an authority on wines, cigars, precious stones and rare books, and was quite an accomplished artist. During his lifetime, he was an enthusiastic photographer and, as a scientist, enjoyed developing and printing his own pictures, including colour photographs.

Even though he was such an eminent scientist, Norman was intrigued by the mysteries of Celtic folklore and the supernatural; he even believed in the existence of the Loch Ness monster!

He is renowned for his story about the legendary Big Grey Man of Ben MacDhui in the Highlands. Mythology suggests that a big grey man frequents the vicinity of Cairngorm's highest summit. Norman's extraordinary encounter took place in 1891 when he was descending from the top on his own in mist and snow. As he walked downhill, he was aware of somebody or something walking behind him but couldn't see who or what it was. For every three or four steps Norman took, the 'being' behind him took just one. When Norman suddenly stopped, so did the steps!

He was so unsettled that he went back up to the summit – the steps followed him. Norman was terrified and ran downhill for eight kilometres until he was safely off the mountain. The report of his encounter generated a lot of press attention when the event was eventually revealed some 26 years later.

In 1929, Norman retired from his university position to spend most of his time on the Isle of Skye. In 1933, his lifelong mountaineering friend on the island, John Mackenzie, died. After he passed away, it is said that Norman made one last solo climb up Am Bastier in the Cuillins then never climbed again.

Norman died in 1942, bringing to an end an extraordinary life in the mountains. John and Norman are buried alongside each other on the Isle of Skye beneath the Cuillin Mountains.

Nanga Parbat, Himalayan Mountains

*Norman standing with his lifelong climbing friend
John Mackenzie*

Present day bronze statue of the two climbing friends at Sligachan on Skye

The Professor of Organic Chemistry at work

Tower Ridge in winter, Ben Nevis

Chapter 14

Knud Rasmussen

Knud Rasmussen

I see only the white desert, the glacier, which draws in deathly cold and blinding snowstorms. There is a seriousness about these vast wastelands.

Knud Rasmussen was a Greenlandic-Dane who travelled across the Inuit lands in the far northern reaches of the world during the early 1900s. He investigated and documented aspects of the Inuit language, traditions and customs. Knud is famous for completing the longest single journey ever made by dogsled.

Early years

Knud was born in 1879 in Illulissat in Western Greenland; he had a Danish missionary father and an Inuit-Danish mother. All his family spoke Inuit and Knud learned the language before he learned Danish.

From an early age he loved to listen to traditional Inuit stories that had been handed down over generations. Like all Greenland children, he learned to hunt, drive dog sleds and to survive in the harsh Arctic environment. He preferred learning about polar skills in the outdoors rather than his more conventional schooling in his missionary home.

When Knud was twelve he left Greenland and went to a boarding school in Copenhagen, Denmark. He found this new environment very strange with its mass of people, buildings, unusual clothes, trees and warm climate. He found the regime of formal learning quite challenging and missed the freedom of his previous life.

After he finished school, Knud studied for a short time at university then tried his hand at acting and opera singing before turning to journalism. A sociable and confident individual who was keen to investigate and research, this line of work suited him. As a journalist he managed to join a student trip travelling to Iceland and also went to northern Scandinavia and wrote about the Sami people.

Returning to Greenland

As a fluent Inuit speaker, Knud had the good fortune to be invited on the Danish Literary Expedition, which was planning to travel across Greenland to study Inuit culture. A policy of isolationism had been adopted by Greenland's Danish colonial government to protect the indigenous population; the Danish Literary Expedition of 1902 was the first of its kind to record aspects of Inuit stories, legends and beliefs.

The expedition comprised both Danes and Greenlanders, and they used Knud's old home in Illulissat as a base where they organised sleds, dogs, polar clothing and other supplies and taught the Danes to drive dogsleds.

Once on their way, they travelled to Upernavik, then the most northerly point of Danish Greenland, where they stayed for the winter. When spring arrived, they went north across the frozen sea ice of Melville Bay and eventually came upon abandoned settlements made by the remote Polar Inuit living in the far north. Members of the expedition ceremoniously raised a flag and declared the rarely visited region for Denmark.

Over the following months they lived with these northern Inuit, hunted with them, shared food and learned about their way of life. After many months, and after the sea had frozen over, they travelled to the south of Greenland so the Danes could catch a ship back to Denmark.

The expedition was a success; they had visited people living on the fringes of the known world, claimed a new area of the Arctic for Denmark and amassed a lot of information about the people of the far north. Back in Denmark, Knud wrote a book about the legends and beliefs of the Polar Inuit which was an instant success when it was published, but although he enjoyed the fame and high-life that came from his new status, he longed to return to his northern world.

In 1905 he journeyed to Greenland again on behalf of the Danish government to investigate the possibility of developing reindeer herding. Before returning to Copenhagen, Knud took another long dogsled trip to visit the Inuit of the far north. In 1908, he was again in Greenland carrying out further studies into their culture. He journeyed to northern Greenland once more but also crossed the ice to Canada's Ellesmere Island; there he hunted and collected hundreds of furs, which he took back to Greenland as part of a new venture he was planning.

Returning to Copenhagen, Knud married the talented Danish pianist, Dagmar Anderson. She was also familiar with Greenland because she had worked as a housekeeper in a west coast settlement for two years.

<u>The First Thule Expedition</u>

A short time after their wedding, Knud returned to Greenland while Dagmar remained in Denmark. He and his Danish friend, Peter Freuchen, planned to establish a trading post at a location they named Thule in the north west of the land; this would make it the most northerly trading post in the world. It was their attempt to secure the region for Denmark before foreign parties became interested. The trading post would provide for the welfare of the local people in an attempt to make their challenging lives easier; it would also be a useful base for future geographical, scientific and cultural expeditions across the Arctic for Knud.

In April 1912, Knud and Peter, with two local men, Uvdoriaq and Inukitsoq, set off on the First Thule Expedition, a 1000 kilometre sled journey to north-eastern Peary Land; their intention was to ascertain if Peary Land was an island separated from the rest of Greenland. During the late 1890s the American, Robert Peary, had explored the region during his push to the North Pole and the area had been named after him. The expedition included four sleds, 53 dogs and a mass of supplies.

They kept to the north-west coast for the first part of their journey before turning eastwards towards the glacial interior; they believed that crossing this unexplored ice cap would be a shortcut to their eventual destination. Reaching a height of more than 2000 metres with temperatures regularly dropping to -30 degrees Celsius, they faced considerable challenges. Knud remarked:

I see only the white desert, the glacier, which draws in deathly cold and blinding snowstorms. There is a seriousness about these vast wastelands...Hour after hour without hearing any sound, without seeing any living thing.

After days on the ice, the sleds eventually descended icy slopes that became dangerously steep. Once off the ice cap, they stopped to hunt in order to replenish their food supplies then followed the coast in a northerly direction. Eventually they established that Peary Land was in fact part of Greenland and not a separate island.

The return journey was another difficult undertaking as they crossed the Greenland ice cap again. The four men suffered injuries, some of the dogs died and the food supplies almost ran out. After an extraordinary five-month trip, the beautiful view of Thule eventually came into sight. This was the first time the Greenland ice cap in the inhospitable far north had ever been crossed.

News of the success of their trip gradually spread across Greenland and Denmark and generated a lot of interest. Knud's time back in Denmark was taken up by writing about the expedition, planning further ventures from Thule and spending time with his family. He had three children with his wife, although he also had a number of other relationships during his lifetime especially with Inuit women.

Eventually it was time to return to Greenland, and in April 1917 the Second Thule Expedition was launched to further explore the far north of Greenland and study its geology, botany and archaeology. Members of the party again included both Danes and Inuit, with each person having a number of tasks to perform.

The group followed the coast northwards, discovering and naming new Arctic locations, and the scientists in the group studied aspects of the environment, but during the Arctic summer they encountered difficulties whilst fording the slush and freezing melt waters. Running short of food supplies, they faced other problems as they travelled over the 1200 metre ice cap. Both dogs and humans struggled to haul the sleds over the uneven terrain; as some dogs died from exhaustion, they were fed to the remaining dogs and men. There were human casualties, too: it was suspected that one member of the party was killed by wolves and another died from the extreme Arctic conditions. Although the party amassed considerable scientific information, it was at considerable cost.

A Third Thule Expedition took place in 1919, when supplies were deposited at various locations to prepare for an Arctic expedition planned by Roald Amundsen on a journey by ship from Spitzbergen to Alaska. Dog sleds full of supplies were taken from Thule to various locations as far as Ellesmere Island in Canada, but the expedition was abandoned after Amundsen's ship became stuck in sea-ice.

The Fourth Thule Expedition took Knud to remote and rarely visited Eastern Greenland where he met with local Inuit groups, especially their elderly members, to gather more information about Inuit culture. For days Knud sat and listened to different stories going back over millennia and later wrote them down. His research suggested that all Inuit people had the same roots; many of the cultural traditions and stories from the west of Greenland where he had grown up were similar to those in the north and east of the island.

His next project would be to investigate Inuit peoples even further to the west in Northern Canada, Alaska and Siberia.

The Fifth Thule Expedition

By the autumn of 1921, expedition members had gathered for the Fifth Thule Expedition. Seventy-five dogs and a range of supplies were placed on board the ship *Søkongen*. From the Greenland shores they sailed west across the Davis Strait and into the Hudson Strait. Eventually the party disembarked on an uninhabited island (now called Danish Island) to the north of Hudson Bay. While some members set to work constructing the expedition base, Knud immediately went off to explore this new Arctic land.

He wrote:

I had often imagined the first meeting with the Inuit of the American Continent... I realised that it had come.

After scanning the horizon he made out a line of sleds and hastily urged his dogs towards them.

I had yelled at the dogs in the language of the Greenland Inuit. And, from the expression on a stranger's face, I realised that he had understood what I said...they went wild with delight... There was a shouting and laughing and cracking of jokes.

Knud was overjoyed that the new people could speak the Inuit language, albeit with a different accent.

At their newly constructed base, the expedition members were assigned different tasks to carry out across the region to gather information about this new land. A key aim was to investigate the housing, clothing, cooking methods, hunting techniques and tools the locals used.

To establish their origins, Knud was particularly interested in Inuit songs, dances, stories and ceremonies. Fortunately he met many different Inuit groups as he made sled trips, often in extreme Arctic weather when it was common to encounter blizzards, strong winds and temperatures dropping to -30 degrees Celsius or lower.

Once the visitors had made contact, they stayed with the Inuit for a few days to learn more about their lives. They discovered that these North Canadian Inuit were divided into two distinct groups: one group, as in Greenland, hunted marine creatures, whilst the other consisted of inland dwellers who lived from caribou.

After 18 months, the first part of the expedition came to an end. The ethnographic interviews finished and 32,000 artefacts were packed up ready to be shipped to Copenhagen, including fishing and hunting gear, household goods and cultural items. Most of the members of the expedition left the region to return to Greenland and Denmark.

However, the second part of the expedition was about to begin. Three members planned to carry out further investigations into the Inuit living even further west and make their way by dogsled across the rest of Arctic North America. They intended to travel the entire length of the North-West Passage, a journey that had never been undertaken before.

The group consisted of Knud and two young Greenland Inuit who were keen to travel into these unknown lands. Miteg was a gifted dog handler and his female cousin, Arnarulunguaq, was a skilled seamstress, cook and master snow-hut builder. They had two long sleds carrying half a ton of gear, and twelve dogs. They knew they would be unable to communicate with the outside world for at least a year.

In March 1923, the party headed off in a north-westerly direction. As before, they spent time with the different groups they encountered along the way, and hunted marine creatures, caribou and musk ox to replenish their food stocks.

On reaching the North-West Passage, they travelled due west to the Mackenzie Delta before they entered Alaska. They noticed that the Inuit groups living in the north-western area of North America were becoming less reliant on traditional ways of life, probably because of the influence of people further to the south.

They continued to Point Barrow on the Arctic Ocean coast before ending their journey at Nome on the west coast of Alaska. The three explorers had completed the longest dog sled journey in polar history and were the first to sled the entire length of the North-West Passage.

Before leaving the region, Knud managed to obtain permission from the Russian authorities to meet some of the Siberian Inuit across the Bering Strait. After chartering a schooner from Nome, he was allowed a brief period to talk to them.

He realised he had travelled to the limit of Inuit culture. His conclusion, based on his lengthy research, was that the Inuit shared a language, legends and similar traditions, and had migrated eastwards across the entire polar region. Their culture had originally emerged out of Asia and had spread all the way to Greenland.

After three-and-a-half years, travelling more than 32,000 kilometres and visiting thousands of Inuit, it was time to head home.

Knud wrote:

From the bottom of my heart, I bless the fate that allowed me to be born at a time when Arctic exploration by dogsled was not yet a thing of the past.

His later life

The three members of the expedition journeyed south across North America before travelling to Europe by ship. Having only ever lived in the polar north, Miteg and Arnarulunguaq were amazed at what they saw in the materially developed world of the United States.

The three explorers had become famous and were greeted by the press, academics and prominent people on their way home, including the President of the United States. Knud attended meetings in both the United States and in Europe to discuss his research and his extraordinary polar journeys. In 1929, he was nominated for (but didn't win) the Nobel Prize for Literature for his extensive work in studying Inuit culture.

A Sixth Thule Expedition took place in Eastern Greenland in 1931; the aim was to chart the coast, collect flora and fauna, take temperature readings and carry out archaeological searches. Knud continued to interview local Inuit groups and add details to his research. The expedition travelled by ship and lasted for the duration of the Arctic summer.

The following year, the Seventh Thule Expedition was once again in Eastern Greenland. It was an even bigger affair, with 62 members who carried out cultural research and surveyed sections of the wild and extremely remote coastline. Knud also found suitable locations for an Inuit film he was involved in making.

Unfortunately, he fell ill and was taken by boat to Nuuk on the west coast. He was transferred to Copenhagen by ship, during which time his condition deteriorated. In hospital, he was diagnosed with a rare form of botulism and developed pneumonia. He passed away in December 1933 at the age of 54.

So ended the life of an exceptional Inuit-Danish man from Greenland. His love of polar environments and of the Inuit culture led him to complete journeys across the Arctic world, and his extensive research was hugely important in our anthropological appreciation of the Inuit people. His adventurous journeys in some of the most inhospitable areas of Greenland and North America by dogsled were quite extraordinary. It is fitting that Knud Rasmussen himself became an Arctic legend within his own lifetime.

'Tails Up!' - starting out on a long run on the Fifth Thule Expedition

Amarulunguaq, Rasmussen and Miteq by their sled, Point Barrow, Alaska, near the end of their great sled journey

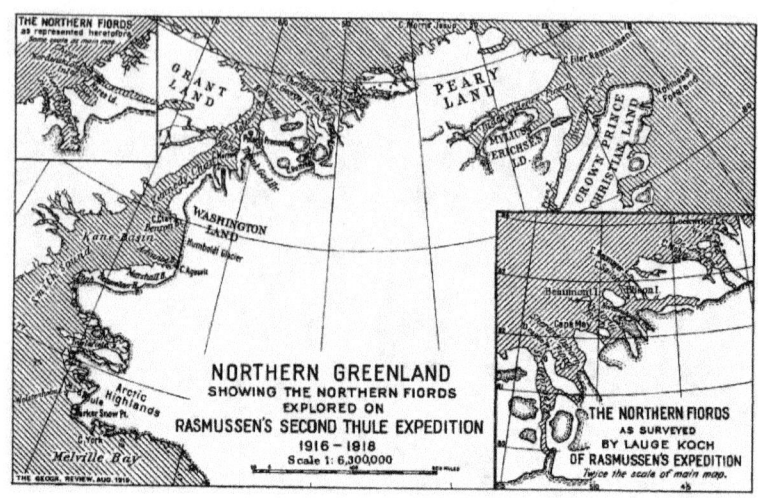

*Map of Northern Greenland and the Second Thule Expedition
1916 – 1918*

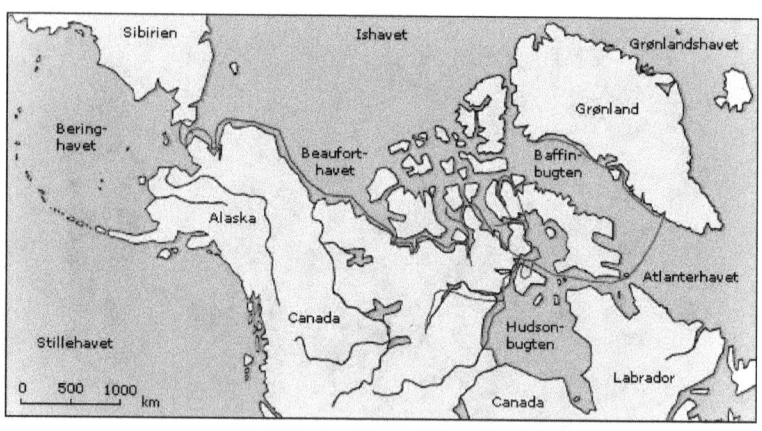

Map of the Fifth Thule Expedition

Members of the Danish Literary Expedition in a snow hut - sketch by Harald Moltke 1902

The Second Thule Expedition

*Travelling camp of the Danish Literary Expedition
- painting by Harold Maltke*

Arnarulunguaq on the Fifth Thule Expedition

'The first man to greet us in these new lands in NE Canada during the Fifth Thule Expedition'

Knud and Inukitsoq consulting a map during the Second Thule Expedition

Chapter 15

Miriam O'Brien Underhill

Miriam O'Brien Underhill

Don't waste time on trivial climbs. You could do the Matterhorn!

Miriam O'Brien Underhill was a gifted American mountaineer at a time of increasing freedom for women in the 1920s and 1930s. She advocated climbing without guides or male companions, which allowed her to take control of the entire experience of scaling a mountain.

Early life

Miriam was born in 1898 in the US state of Maryland. Her father was a newspaper editor and government official and her mother was a physician. As a young child, her favourite activity was tree climbing. When she was six her parents, both lovers of the mountains, took her into the wilds of New Hampshire to the foothills of the White Mountains. For Miriam it was a most memorable occasion:

> *I got my first taste of the wild, uncrowded places of the earth and even at six years old I liked it. For years afterwards I cherished these impressions...*

Throughout her childhood these rugged locations were places she continued to visit. She loved any adventure in these natural environments and the sheer delight of being in the great outdoors.

First visits to the European Alps

As was often the case in affluent families of the time, Miriam was taken on a visit to Europe when she was sixteen years of age. In 1914 she, her mother and her younger brother, Lincoln, who was then seven, visited both Chamonix and Zermatt in the Alps. Whilst in Chamonix, Miriam and her mother trekked to the top of the 2525 metre high Le Brévent overlooking the deep glacial valley, and feasted upon the breathtaking view of Mont Blanc. Looking across at the mountain vista with its many neighbouring jagged summits was completely overwhelming.

Later on, whilst the family were staying with friends in Switzerland, World War One broke out and they found themselves stranded in the country until transport could be arranged to take them home. Having time on their hands, they journeyed to Zermatt to hike and admire the sights of the Matterhorn, together with many other renowned peaks.

On a little train from Visp, we rounded that last corner and the Matterhorn came into view, it took my breath away that first time as it has so often since.

After the war Miriam returned to the Alps several times to hike and climb some of the more straightforward summits. Back in the United States, she joined the Appalachian Mountain Club where she developed her mountaineering skills.

Her prowess as a rock climber impressed certain members of this enthusiastic group and she was invited on some demanding trips to the White Mountains of New Hampshire, particularly during winter. During such excursions, Miriam walked and climbed in all weathers, skied on wooden skis and snowshoed.

Tackling harder climbs

It was suggested that Miriam could climb far more demanding routes than she had been doing. In a mountain hut in the Swiss Alps, George Finch, a member of the 1922 Everest expedition, told her: *'Don't waste time on trivial climbs. You could do the Matterhorn!'*

That comment was a turning point in her mountaineering career. Two days later she traversed the Zermatt peaks of Wellenkuppe and Obergabelhorn, both around 4,000 metres.

Returning to the Alps in 1926, she was determined to tackle more demanding routes. When visiting the Dolomites in the Italian Alps, she enjoyed some of the most exciting climbing she had ever done. Miriam loved the long, steep, exposed conditions that required small toe and finger holds and a delicate sense of balance.

The following year, climbing with a guide, she made the first-ever ascent of the route Via Miriam on the Torre Grande, which was named in her honour. That same season she went to the French Alps to Chamonix and, with a guide, completed the first ascent of the sheer, exposed pinnacle Aiguille de Roc at 3407 metres. That climb was soon followed by an ascent of the Grépon, the first female ascent of what was considered to be one of the most challenging climbs in the Alps.

Miriam was now climbing to a very high standard; she gained a reputation throughout the Alps and certainly raised a few eyebrows in some sections of the climbing fraternity.

During this time, she took winter trips to the Alps where she completed a number of ski mountaineering tours. She skied with local guide friends and other acquaintances with whom she had climbed during her summer trips. These winter excursions involved ascending summits in both the French and the Swiss Alps before skiing down, often in extreme weather. Skiing down glaciers was fraught with danger!

In 1928, she completed another alpine first with two guides and Robert Underhill, her future husband. They traversed all five pinnacles of the Aiguilles du Diable, each at a height above 4000 metres. The climb took 18 hours to complete and was exceptionally difficult. Then, to prove to herself that she could climb as well as anyone else, she took the lead on the Grépon with a guide acting as the second climber. This was the first time an ascent of this prestigious route had been led by a woman.

'Manless' climbing

Miriam had become increasingly convinced that in order to obtain the greatest satisfaction as a climber she needed to climb without a guide. She believed that if a person always follows a good leader they miss out on many of the delights and rewards of climbing; the ultimate fulfilment must be to control the entire experience, including route finding, solving any problems and reacting to an emergency. She was also convinced that this should be without any men in the party so they would not be tempted to take over if problems arose. Miriam came up with the phrase of 'manless' climbing; it was her attempt at rebelling against the chauvinism and narrow-mindedness in society at the time.

On her return to the Alps In 1929, it was time to try out her revolutionary ideas. With Winifred Marples from Britain she completed the first manless ascent of the Aiguille du Peigne in the Mont Blanc range.

Three days later, Miriam paired up with the French climber Alice Damesme and prepared to climb the Grépon. They took it in turns to lead the various sections of this technically testing, exposed and strenuous climb. They succeeded and received great acclaim from some but, sadly, considerable ridicule from other quarters. One professional guide commented:

'The Grépon has disappeared. Now that it has been done by two women alone, no self-respecting man can undertake it. A pity, too, because it used to be a very good climb.'

Ignoring such an insult, Miriam began planning the first manless climb of the Matterhorn, arguably the most famed of all mountains.

At the beginning of the 1931 season, Miriam and Micheline Morin, a French mountaineer, made manless ascents of the Jungfrau and the Mönch. Later on, climbing with fellow American, Jessie Whitehead, she completed the Zermatt peak of Alphubel. These peaks were suitable training for the Matterhorn, with each being over 4000 metres in height.

Unfortunately, Miriam's climbing plans were dashed when poor weather put paid to any attempt that year. The following season, on the 12th of August, Miriam and Alice fulfilled their dream and made the first ever manless ascent of the famous mountain. They climbed the Hörnli Ridge in good time and without a hitch.

A big celebration was due to take place to mark this first 'women only' Matterhorn ascent – but instead of partying, Miriam and Robert Underhill went off climbing in the Eastern Alps.

Later years

Miriam had proved that, given the opportunity, women could equal men in mountaineering. Miriam and Robert eventually married back in the United States and climbed, hiked and skied together. If any rock or ice climbing was involved, they shared the lead and worked as equals.

They had two sons and, as soon as possible, they were also introduced to the mountains. Miriam and Robert explored and climbed the wilder parts of the United States including trips to the mountains of Idaho, Montana and Wyoming, where they made numerous first ascents. In 1939 they climbed Miriam Peak in Wyoming (3989 metres), which was named in her honour.

In 1952, Miriam and Robert returned to the Alps and climbed the Matterhorn together. They continued to be active in the Appalachian Mountain Club and devised an interesting challenge for their fellow members: to climb each of the forty-eight 4000-foot (1219 metre) high peaks, during the months of winter. Unsurprisingly, Miriam and Robert were the first to complete this gruelling, severe-weather challenge and climbed their final peak, Mount Jefferson, on New Year's Eve 1961; Miriam was 62 and Robert was 71. She was also the first person to ascend all 100 of New England's highest peaks.

Miriam died in 1976 aged seventy-seven. She had become an extraordinary mountaineer and a strong proponent of both guideless and women-only mountaineering. She had discredited the common belief of the time that women had neither the physical nor mental capability to lead challenging climbs and has been an inspiration for generations of women who have climbed in her footsteps.

Aiguille du Grépon (Credit: Simo Räsänen)

Mount Washington, the highest of the Four Thousand Footers (Credit: Harvey Barrison)

The Matterhorn (Credit: Matterhorn Museum Zermatt)

*Bobs Tower and Mariam Peak in Wyoming
(Credit: SummitPost)*

Miriam climbing in the Alps

Miriam O'Brien Underhill

Chapter 16

Isobel Wylie Hutchison

Isobel Wylie Hutchinson

*I must go North again! My heart
Is where the white mist lies*

Isobel was an Arctic traveller during the 1920s and 1930s. She was also a botanist, a writer, a poet, an artist and speaker of many languages including Gaelic, Icelandic and Inuit.

Early life

Isobel was born in Carlowrie Castle near Edinburgh, in 1889. She was the third of five children born into a family of successful Scottish wine merchants. As a child, she enjoyed gardening and learning about the plants in her large garden with her father. During her formal education, her favourite subjects were learning languages and writing both prose and poetry. She was a very active child and enjoyed a number of sports, but her favourite pastime was to go for long walks; as she grew older, her hikes could be as long as 100 to 160 kilometres and take several days to complete.

The serenity of her family's life was shattered in 1912 when her 16-year-old brother, Frank, died in a climbing accident in the Cairngorm Mountains. Three years later her brother Walter died during World War One.

The loss of her two brothers had a huge impact on Isobel. From 1917 to 1918 she studied at an agricultural college in Warwickshire; with her love of plants and gardening, it seemed an obvious career to follow. When she finished her course, she visited various locations around the Mediterranean including the Holy Land, Egypt, Spain, Portugal, France and Morocco.

These visits had a definite structure with little opportunity for independent exploration. This didn't really suit Isobel's free-spirited character; she would have preferred more adventurous trips where she could make her own discoveries and go her own way. With these thoughts in mind, on her return to Scotland she decided to trek up the length of Scotland's Outer Hebrides, some 240 kilometres or so, hopping from island to island.

This was the freedom of travel she preferred: simply carrying a rucksack, walking on her own and making her own way just as she pleased. During her journey she spent her nights in either fishermen's cottages or farmhouses.

The joy of such an independent journey in such northerly locations sowed the seeds for future excursions. Isobel wrote a report of her Hebridean journey which was published in the *National Geographic Magazine*. Her fee for the article helped pay for her next trip to a place even further north.

Iceland and Greenland

In the summer of 1925, unable to resist the lure of venturing ever northward, Isobel decided to travel to Iceland. She went on her own, arranged her travel and decided to simply see where the journey took her. Given the period in which she lived, such independence was very unconventional for a young single woman.

Arriving in Iceland, she spent time walking and using ponies to explore the Reykjavik region, visiting geyser fields and the Hekla Volcano. Wanting to understand the character of this volcanic land, its people and its nature, Isobel then set about planning a more challenging journey. Her idea was to walk from Reykjavik in the south west to the settlement of Akureyri in the very north of the island, a journey of more than 400 kilometres. Local Icelandic acquaintances declared her proposal impossible; she didn't know the way, there were no maps available, many rivers would be too deep to ford and she couldn't speak Icelandic!

Undeterred, Isobel tried to find a local guide to go with her but nobody was available, though one local person did describe the best route to take. She set off alone following tracks and paths, frequently getting lost, often experiencing extreme weather, but arriving at set locations at the end of each day. When she came across rivers too deep to ford, she found help from farmers nearby who provided ponies.

Along the way, Isobel stayed on isolated farms or with church ministers in small settlements. She often helped with farm chores, both to assist the farmers in their toil and as a thank you for their hospitality.

As she sailed out of Akureyri harbour, having succeeded on a seemingly impossible trek, Isobel was already dreaming of her next 'northerly' adventure.

Next she wanted to travel to Greenland, but visiting Denmark's only colony wasn't going to be easy. This huge ice-domed land was heavily protected and practically closed to the outside world; both Danish citizens and foreigners had great difficulty in visiting the colony. With very few visitors, Greenland was largely an unknown entity and held a great deal of mystery and intrigue for the outside world. For Isobel, this added to its appeal.

Amongst the island's trickle of visitors each year were Danish government officials, clergy and scientists. Realising this, Isobel decided to apply to visit Greenland as a private botanist in order to collect plants. Her initial application was rejected by officials in Copenhagen so she applied again. Whilst awaiting a reply, she set about finding out all she could about the country as well as learning the Danish language. She also organised a visit to the Lofoten Islands in the north of Norway where she walked, climbed and generally explored.

In 1927 Isobel successfully obtained permission to visit Greenland as a botanist. Travelling by supply ship from Denmark, she went first to the settlement of Angmagssalik in the east of the island. She ventured forth in Inuit kayak and *umiak* boats to visit local tented villages, to collect plants and generally admire all she saw around her.

It was summertime and Isobel hadn't realised that biting insects would be so troublesome. This problem was largely solved when she obtained a pair of local knee-length boots or *kamiker* that prevented insects from attacking any exposed flesh.

Moving to the southern part of the island, she explored various regions by *umiak*, stayed in local settlements, learned about the lives of the people who lived there and added to her plant collection. After five months in Greenland, she returned to Scotland but rapidly applied to return.

Her visit had consolidated her growing love for far northerly locations, as is evident in her poem *Call of the North:*

I must go North again! My heart
Is where the white mist lies
About the roots of starlit crags
Beneath the Arctic skies,
Where through the dusk the Dancers play
Across the northern pole;
I must go North again, for they
Have stolen away my soul.

Isobel's request was successful and in the summer of 1928 she travelled to the west of Greenland where she planned to overwinter. She started her visit in the Umanak area, halfway up the west coast of the island and well inside the Arctic Circle. Again she planned to collect as many plant specimens as possible but snow increasingly covered the land, the temperatures dropped and the long Arctic night began.

From October to April, the sun sank beneath the horizon and the local bay was frozen. Isabel spent her days living and learning amongst the Greenlandic people and Danish officials. When the sun re-appeared, she travelled through this coastal region and stayed with the indigenous people; by this stage, she was fluent in the Inuit language.

When the summer arrived and more snow started to melt, Isobel decided to climb one of the highest peaks in northwestern Greenland, Qilertinguit, which was around 2000 metres in height. The mountain had been climbed only twice before and she had been watching it all through her stay in the area. She travelled with two Inuit men; they stayed in a rudimentary sod hut and Isobel in a tent.

They waited three days in freezing winds for the weather to improve and, as the storm abated, they set off. After climbing up shale and snow, they used a rope for the top section before successfully reaching the summit at 9.30pm. On the top of Qilertinguit they found a bottle inside a cairn and added their names to it. It was a most wonderful occasion as they watched the Arctic summer light illuminate the Greenland landscape.

The North American Arctic

By now Isobel was making a name for herself as a traveller of the Far North. She had written books about her experiences in both Iceland and Greenland and was increasingly in demand to give talks about her Arctic journeys. However, she still wanted to discover more of these northerly destinations, so she made enquiries about journeys to Arctic Canada, Alaska and Siberia.

Making arrangements wasn't easy, particularly if she wished to travel into the Russian Arctic, but eventually she arranged to travel to Alaska and Northern Canada to explore and collect plant specimens.

In May 1933, Isobel left Manchester and went by ship, river-boat, train and plane to Nome in Alaska. Once there, she planned to travel to Barrow, the most northerly settlement in the United States then make her way along the north Alaskan coast where she would overwinter on Herschel Island. At the time Alaska had a pioneering atmosphere and was inhabited by both local Inuit and outsiders trying to make whatever living they could in such a harsh and often frozen environment.

Isobel obtained a passage on a small trading ship that gradually made its way along the coast taking supplies to local Inuit villages. The journey was often interrupted by storms, heavy seas and pack ice, which made it impossible to travel. This gave her the opportunity to go ashore to walk, explore and collect plant specimens.

Eventually she arrived in Barrow where she transferred to another small vessel owned by Gus Masik, an Estonian migrant who had escaped the turmoil of the Russian Revolution and ended up in Alaska working as a sailor, trader, trapper and prospector. Unfortunately, even though it was mid-September, the Arctic Ocean ice was closing in and making it impossible to travel any further by boat. They were forced to retreat to Gus's one-room cabin where Isobel stayed for many weeks until the weather situation improved.

Although her journey had come to a halt, it was an opportunity to visit local Inuit families, walk, travel by dogsled and overnight in igloos. Eventually, Isobel continued her Arctic adventure with a 200 kilometre sled journey and crossed into Canada at Demarcation Point.

On her way Isobel described entering an igloo:

...amid the snow and ice-bergs that covered the sea rose the fairy like dome of a snow- house...Crawling on hands and knees through the low doorway, I found myself in a tiny crystal chamber, its wall, floor and roof shining like diamonds in the light of a candle frozen to the floor.

Her trip took her to Herschel Island then on to Aklavik on the Mackenzie River. After many months in the Alaskan and Canadian Arctic she returned to Scotland, having been away for about a year.

Unable to obtain permission from the Soviet authorities to visit Eastern Siberia, Isobel's next northerly journey was in 1936 to the Aleutian Islands, off the coast of Alaska. This thousand-mile archipelago of large and small volcanic islands is draped like a gigantic necklace between Alaska and the Kamchatka Peninsula in the far east of the USSR. The islands were inhabited by Aleut people who were living on treeless terrain exposed to continuous windy, foggy and stormy weather.

> *Here undoubtedly was where the storms are born. Here is the cradle of the tempests. For storms, all you need is air masses at different temperatures...On one side...was the Pacific Ocean...on the other...the Arctic current...the heavy cold air of the Bering pours to meet the rising air of the Pacific...*

The Aleut people were able to live in such extreme conditions because of the abundance of sea creatures that provided for their needs. Once again Isobel was allowed to visit this isolated region in order to collect plant specimens. Arriving on one of the larger islands, Unalaska, Isobel planned to befriend any vessel that could take her to other islands. Fortunately, she was able to visit many of the inhabited islands by way of US coast guard and government fisheries vessels.

Landing on the islands invariably involved negotiating heavy seas in extreme weather but when she did make land she met the local inhabitants, explored and collected huge numbers of plant specimens.

Isobel described one of her visits as hurricane-force winds raged:

> *I experienced the curiously exhilarating sensation of literally wrestling with the wind, and the wind won easily, lifting me right off my feet several times, so that I was obliged to hold on to the mountain-side by hands and knees.*

Fortunately, she was able to reach many islands including the most westerly of the Aleutian chain, Attu Island. This was the last, rarely visited American outpost before entering Soviet Russia.

Later years

The onset of the Second World War curtailed Isobel's plans for further journeys into the Arctic but she continued to write books and articles about her exploits as well as publish poetry.

She was also in demand as a public speaker and made radio broadcasts for the BBC.

After the war Isobel made a number of trips to Europe. Her love of hiking continued and she completed long treks, including walking from her home in Scotland to London, from Innsbruck to Venice, and from Edinburgh to John O'Groats.

Isobel Wylie Hutchison died at her home in Carlowrie Castle in 1982 aged 92. It was the end of a life of great passion for far northerly lands.

During Isobel's journey across Alaska with Gus Masik, Sandspit Island (Credit: Royal Scottish Geographical Society)

Isobel Wylie Hutchinson wearing traditional Greenland clothing (Credit: Royal Scottish Geographical Society)

Greenland umiak boat (Credit: Carl Rasmussen)

Inuit harpooning a whale, Point Barrow, Alaska

Chapter 17

Alexandra David-Néel

Alexandria David-Neel

I craved to go beyond the garden gate...and set out for the Unknown.

Alexandra David-Néel was a keen adventurer who travelled through Asia during the first part of the twentieth century. Her extraordinary journeying took her across China, India and into the secret world of Tibet.

Earlier life

Alexandra was born in Paris in 1868. Her father was a French journalist and teacher, and her mother was a native of Belgium.

From an early age she possessed an adventurous spirit and a desire to explore the world, though her upbringing was very strict and uneventful. She once wrote about her childhood years:

> *I craved to go beyond the garden gate…and set out for the Unknown.*

As she grew older, her passion for adventure increased. As a teenager, Alexandra managed to board a train that took her first to Switzerland and then into Italy before her mother caught up with her and took her back home to Brussels.

In 1886, when she was just 18 years of age, Alexandra tied a few belongings to her bicycle and set off on another lone trip without informing her parents. She cycled all the way from her home in Belgium to Spain before returning via the French Riviera and back through the Alps. A cycling trip on mostly dirt roads was a daring act for a female to carry out alone during the late 1800s, and her bold, free-thinking spirit was deemed scandalous. She also spent time in London where she studied English and Asian religions; so began her fascination with the East.

In 1889 she moved to Paris where she learned more about Asian religions and started learning both the Sanskrit and Tibetan languages. In the same year she decided to become a Buddhist. In 1890, once again travelling alone, she visited India and Ceylon until she ran out of the inheritance money she had been given.

Returning to Europe, she began writing articles about her travels but soon realised that, as a woman, she would have difficulties in making a living. Instead, she turned to professional singing where she believed she might find more success.

Between 1895 and 1904, Alexandra was immersed in the world of opera. After studying piano and singing at the Royal Conservatory of Brussels, she became an opera singer. She was a gifted performer and found work in a number of French colonies, including at the Hanoi Opera House. She co-wrote an opera in Paris and performed in Athens and Tunis. During her stay in Tunis she met Philippe Néel, an engineer for the Tunisian Railways, and they married in 1904.

A journey to Tibet

Alexandra found it difficult to shake off her fascination with Asia and had an overwhelming urge to return. Her husband was quite willing to support his wife's desire to learn more about the East, so in 1911 she went on another lone journey to India to continue her religious studies.

In India she met with the thirteenth Dalai Lama before travelling to the Himalayan kingdom of Sikkim where she studied aspects of Buddhism with the Crown Prince of this small Himalayan nation. Alexandra eventually travelled north and lived in a cave for two years in order to achieve Buddhist enlightenment. The cave was situated about 4000 metres up a mountain in northern Sikkim, close to the Tibetan border. She lived alone; her only visitor was an aide who brought her one meal every day. The assistant was a 15-year-old Sikkimese monk called Aphur Yongden, whom she later adopted. Alexandra was eventually ordained as a Tibetan Buddhist lama.

At the end of her time in the cave, Alexandra decided to visit Tibet even though it had been out of bounds to foreign visitors for decades because of a fear of the country being overrun by the Russian and British empires. This did not deter her, and in 1916 she and Aphur started a brief, illegal trek into the country, staying at a number of religious locations within this mountainous land.

On her return to Sikkim, the colonial British authorities were so incensed with her having ignored the ban on entering Tibet that she and Aphur were deported.

Deciding where to travel was a huge problem: returning to Europe would have been nigh on impossible as it was now the height of the First World War. Instead they chose to travel to Japan and Korea, then made their way through China from east to west through a country that was collapsing into civil war. It was a journey of more than 3000 kilometres, most of which they completed on foot. The pair witnessed murders, battles and were often confronted by warlords; they walked through dense forests, barren lands, in great heat and freezing temperatures.

Eventually they reached Mongolia and crossed the Gobi Desert. Both of them became seriously ill and were suffering from malnutrition, but eventually they reached the Kumbum Monastery in eastern Tibet. Alexandra spent many months at this sanctuary translating religious scripts with Aphur's help.

Unsurprisingly, she started to think about visiting Llasa, the holiest of Buddhist cities. This meant venturing deep into Tibet; if she was successful, she would be the first Western woman to visit this forbidden city. It was an ambitious idea and required considerable planning but the journey might just be feasible if Alexandra and Aphur travelled disguised as a Buddhist lama and his ageing mother. By now Alexandra could speak fluent Tibetan and was familiar with most cultural aspects of the area. She blackened her hair with Chinese ink and added a yak's tail to lengthen it, then darkened her face and hands each day with soot from the bottom of their cooking pot. The 'make-up skills' learnt from her opera singing days were coming in useful!

Carrying only the bare minimum of luggage, they started their journey. Beneath their garments they carried valuables including money, a compass and pistols, the latter only to be used if they met bandits who wanted to harm them.

After crossing the Mekong River they headed west towards Lhasa via the Dokar Pass through the Kha Karpo Mountains. Alexandra wrote:

'How happy I was to be there, en route for these unexplored heights, alone in the great silence...'

Their path was continually patrolled by soldiers on horseback who were on the lookout for foreigners and undesirables. The pair preferred to walk in the dark to avoid contact with too many people; by day they slept in out-of-the-way locations after pitching their small tent, or sheltering inside caves.

Inevitably there were occasions when they met others. Travelling as pilgrims, they would ask for directions so they might continue their journey; in return the Tibetans would demand to have their fortunes told by the travellers, or have their demons exorcised.

Some of the most demanding and dangerous parts of their Himalayan trek were when they crossed mountain rivers. On one occasion they needed to cross a fast-flowing torrent in a deep gorge. Alexandra and a young Tibetan girl were tethered together in a basket and hauled across a deep chasm by a simple pulley. Unfortunately the leather cable they were using to pull them across suddenly snapped and the basket slid back into the centre of the sagging ropeway; they were in danger of crashing down into the flowing water far below. Eventually, the pair were rescued by a workman who crawled upside down to repair the cableway.

On other occasions it was the deep snow, high passes and indistinct paths that were problematic. It once took practically 24 hours to ascend a snow-filled, almost 6000 metre high mountain pass without any food or suitable place to rest. Although suffering, Alexandra took time to reflect:

...the scenery was grand beyond all description...the moon rose...its rays touched the glaciers and high snow-robed peaks...

On another occasion an avalanche of snow almost buried their tent whilst they slept inside, totally exhausted. Later still, after falling into a deep snow hole Aphur sprained his ankle and had to rest up in a cave. They were both worn out and in serious need of something substantial to eat. Such was their hunger, they were forced to boil their yak-hide boot leather to eat.

After many trying days, they found themselves in easier terrain walking along valleys – but thieves were preying on pilgrims! The pair were confronted by a band of robbers and had to brandish their pistols. After that encounter they were set upon by ferocious dogs, but they continued in the knowledge their journey was coming to an end.

As they neared their destination, they were pleased to mingle unnoticed with other travellers along the road heading to the city. Finally, after four months of exhausting travel, they reached Lhasa where they remained for two months, taking sanctuary in a number of monasteries.

Eventually, the authorities found out about their presence in the city but luckily by this time they had already left. Alexandra and Aphur managed to reach Northern India via Sikkim.

Alexandra decided it was time to go back to Europe. What had initially been planned as a short trip lasting only a few months had lasted for fourteen years!

Later life

By the time she returned to France in 1925, Alexandra was a national celebrity. Newspapers and magazines had written enthusiastic accounts of her travels.

On her return, Alexandra and her husband Philippe, whom she had not lived with for such a long time, decided to part company. She and Aphur settled in the town of Dignes-les-Bains in Provence in south-west France. During the following years she wrote several books about her journeys through India, China and Tibet and also about Buddhism and the way of life she had adopted. As a consequence, her notoriety as an adventurer and religious scholar grew in the francophone world and beyond.

However the desire to continue journeying in the East was too great. In 1937, aged 69, Alexandra and Aphur decided to return to China. From Brussels they travelled to Moscow, then to China on the Trans-Siberian Railway. They arrived at a time of great unrest in the middle of the Chinese-Japanese war; it took them one and a half years to cross a country in turmoil amidst violence, famine and epidemics, mainly on foot.

In 1938 they crossed back into Tibet and found sanctuary in the town of Tachienlu, where they stayed for the next five years. They eventually went to India and returned to France in 1946.

They settled back into their French home where Alexandra, now 78, continued writing; in total, she published more than 30 books during her lifetime. In 1955 her adopted son and travelling companion, Aphur, died.

At the age of 100, Alexandra applied for a new passport with a view of returning to Tibet but she passed away a few months later in 1969. Her and Aphur's ashes were eventually taken and poured into the River Ganges.

Alexandra David-Néel's life has been celebrated in a variety of ways with plays, documentaries and films. Most fitting of all perhaps, given her earlier life, an opera was written about her. She surely must be one of the most extraordinary adventurers in recent history.

*Lama Aphur Yongden, Alexandra David-Néel
and a young pilgrim outside Lhasa*

Lhasa 1905

Alexandra with Lama Aphur Yongden

Performing in an opera around 1900, stage name Alexandra Myrial

Alexandra David-Néel

Chapter 18

Alain Gerbault

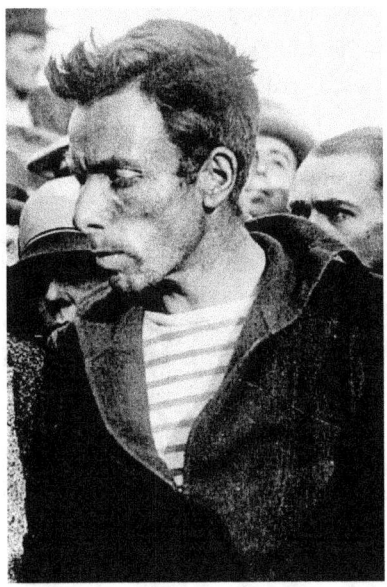

Alain Gerbault

Suddenly I saw… a huge wave rearing its curling snowy crest so high that it dwarfed all others I had ever seen. I could hardly believe my eyes.

Alain Gerbault made a solo circumnavigation of the world in a yacht during the 1920s. He was the third person to achieve this daring feat. Alain was also an international tennis player, a writer, and he became a spokesperson for indigenous Pacific Islanders.

Early years

Alain Gerbault was born in 1893 in Laval, western France, into a well-off family; his father was a successful industrialist. When he was young he spent a lot of time near the sea not far from St Malo in Brittany.

Alain sailed with his father, who owned a boat, and made friends with the local Breton fishermen. He spent time reading books about sea adventures and steadily became more and more fascinated with seafaring; he dreamed of the day he would have his own boat.

As a teenager he played football and tennis, and when he was older he started training to be a civil engineer. When the First World War broke out Alain joined the Flying Corps', 'Squadron of Wolves' and by the end of the hostilities he was a decorated war hero.

During the 1920s and 1930s, he played in numerous international tennis tournaments and became quite a sports star; by 1893, he was ranked fifth male player in France, and took part in the French and US Opens and Wimbledon.

Whilst visiting Britain, Alain bought something that enhanced his love of the sea: a 12 metre racing yacht called *Firecrest*. He spent more than a year learning how to sail his new craft around the French Riviera and also competed in tennis tournaments.

He had been considering making a long sea journey for some time, and as he sailed his new boat he tested himself to prove that he was capable of such an ambitious undertaking:

During more than a year I trained physically, cruising in all sorts of weather, learning how to handle my sails alone. Only when I felt myself ready, when I knew that I could stand the mental and physical strain, did I start on my cruise.

Finally he was prepared for a sea adventure. His aim was to sail across the Atlantic Ocean, a plan that had first been formulated with two of his comrades during the war. Sadly they had both died so Alain decided to sail alone.

Crossing the Atlantic Ocean

Alain left Cannes in the south of France in April 1923 and headed for Gibraltar. It was a challenging trip and storms damaged his yacht. After some much-needed repairs and alterations to *Firecrest*, he continued his journey. If he succeeded, it would be the first-ever single-handed sailing from east to west across the Atlantic!

He established a daily routine, selecting the correct sails for the conditions, navigating, and cooking in a limited space. The seas were so heavy that it was often necessary to spend as much as twelve hours a day steering the vessel. During more settled periods, Alain repaired any equipment, including sewing sails, and found time to read some of the many books he had brought aboard *Firecrest*.

Several weeks after starting his journey, and with over 4000 kilometres to sail before he arrived in the United States, he discovered that the fresh water on board was contaminated. After some calculations, he decided to ration himself to half a glass of water per day, though this was a problem because the weather became very hot. He developed a fever and his throat became swollen.

He then found that the salted beef he was carrying was inedible, so he threw it overboard for the creatures below. The two stoves on *Firecrest* stopped working, though with some considerable effort he managed to repair one of them.

After a couple of weeks of water rationing, he started to catch rain in a sail. At first he only collected a little, but as the rain grew heavier he was able to stop rationing. He substituted flying fish that jumped aboard the boat for the beef he had lost, and discovered that if he dangled his feet in the sea as bait, he could catch fish!

Further across the Atlantic, Alain met hurricane-force winds and wild seas. He wrote in his log:

Suddenly I saw...a huge wave rearing its curling snowy crest so high that it dwarfed all others I had ever seen. I could hardly believe my eyes...Knowing that if I stayed on deck I would meet death by being washed overboard, I had just time to climb into the rigging, and was about half-way to the masthead when it burst upon the Firecrest in fury...my sails cannot stand the strain...It is now a real hurricane.

The yacht continually faced an onslaught of massive waves that engulfed its deck in tons of water, and Alain spent a lot of time repairing sails and rigging. Because of the amount work he had to undertake, he lost many nights' sleep; neither could he eat much because his two stoves continued to malfunction. After twenty days of devastating weather, below deck was awash with sea-water.

Calmer conditions eventually ensued, producing a number of days of mist where Alain had to give regular blasts of the *Firecrest*'s foghorn – there were a number of trans-Atlantic steamers to avoid! Finally, on the morning of September 15th, he reached New York having spent a total of 101 days crossing the Atlantic Ocean. He had completed the first, non-stop solo crossing by yacht from east to west!

Alain decided to completely refurbish the *Firecrest*. Having spent many weeks in a range of sea conditions, he'd had time to identify what parts of the craft needed adapting, improving or replacing. Most importantly, he had also taken the decision to continue sailing his vessel into new waters and to journey around the whole world! Before departing, however, he took part in the Davis Cup tennis match being held in the city.

The Pacific Ocean

Two days out from New York, in night-time conditions, the *Firecrest* almost collided with a steamer! The larger vessel probably didn't see the smaller craft in the dark and scraped along the side of Alain's yacht, causing considerable damage that he had to repair the best he could.

Next, he was again battered by gales; within two weeks of leaving New York, much of the refit of *Firecrest* had been wrecked. Alain made for Bermuda where his yacht underwent yet more repairs.

After three months he sailed without incident to Colon, the Atlantic entrance to the Panama Canal. As was the custom, his yacht was towed the length of the canal to Bilboa on the Pacific Ocean side. There Alain decided to take part in the Panama Tennis Championship, which he won! Indeed, wherever he landed he always tried to play tennis or football to keep himself fit.

Firecrest headed south west to the Galápagos Islands but it took over a month to cover around 1300 kilometres because of adverse currents. Arriving at the islands, Alain stocked up on fresh water and fruit for his next leg, a journey of over 4800 kilometres to Tahiti – during which further problems developed with *Firecrest*'s sailing gear. When he arrived on Wallis Island in French Polynesia, the anchor failed to hold the yacht and the vessel was embedded in sand, seriously damaging the keel.

I had been an hour on the reef when suddenly my boat keeled right over on to one side, the deck became almost vertical, and the water began to pour in at the skylight...

Alain lived on his yacht as he sought help to carry out the repairs. He spent a lot of his time with the indigenous islanders and learned their language; this made him very popular with the locals and he gradually developed a strong bond with the Polynesians, their culture and their way of life.

With the assistance of workers from a French naval vessel, *Firecrest* was eventually repaired and ready to continue the journey across the Pacific. Once Alain reached the port of Suva in Fiji, he was able to make more necessary repairs to his yacht before sailing to New Guinea through the Torres Strait north of Australia, then out into the Indian Ocean.

Firecrest's completed circumnavigation

Alain sailed to the Keeling Islands, then to Mauritius and the island of Reunion. As he travelled towards Durban in South Africa, *Firecrest* was exposed to more stormy conditions. Further along the coast, he put his boat into dry dock at Cape Town where he discovered teredo sea worms had eaten away part of the rudder!

After rounding the Cape of Good Hope, Alain entered the Atlantic Ocean and set sail in a northerly direction. He sailed across the southern Atlantic to St Helena and then to Ascension Island before taking on headwinds on his way to the Cape Verde Islands. Unfortunately, the side of the *Firecrest* was holed as a result of it being too close to a reef so more repairs were required, this time on the island of São Vicente.

During the last leg of the journey as he headed towards France, Alain was forced to continually use the yacht's pump as *Firecrest* was taking in water through the hole it had received.

As the end of my voyage drew nearer a great sadness took possession of me; the cruise was soon to end, and with it the happiest period of my life...

In May 1929, Alain entered the port of Le Havre, having successfully circumnavigated the globe in his yacht. He was given a warm reception and, in celebration of his extraordinary feat, was presented with a gold medal and made an Officer of the Legion of Honour!

The journey had lasted more than six years and Alain had covered nearly 65,000 kilometres. He was the third person to make a solo journey around the world in a boat and had proved himself to be a competent seafarer and skilled navigator. It has been suggested that a person with less persistence, resolve and physical fitness would have given up on what turned out to be an incredibly challenging trip.

His later years

After the euphoria of his success, Alain thought about what he should do with the rest of his life. He realised that he missed life at sea and in particular the time he had spent with the people of the Pacific. As he assessed his future he wrote:

Although man has been accustomed to living as a slave to civilization for centuries, I will not be forced to lead the same servile and conventional life.

Alain decided to return to the islands of the Pacific Ocean, again by boat. He knew that *Firecrest* was worn out and would not make the journey – the ageing craft had too many parts which needed constant repair – so he built a new, smaller yacht measuring just over 10 metres. This was completed by 1931 and named the *Alain Gerbault*.

The great circumnavigator sailed away, once more single-handedly, to live in the islands he had become so attached to. Gradually he vanished from the public eye as he wandered from island to island in the Pacific aboard his new vessel. As he travelled, he wrote extensively about the history and society of French Polynesia and published several books in which he frequently criticised the colonial exploitation that he saw wherever he journeyed.

After catching malaria, Alain Gerbault passed away in 1941 at the age of 48, in Dili, East Timor. A monument to this great friend of the Pacific was built on the French Polynesian island of Bora Bora.

Alain was an extraordinary adventurer, famed for completing a solo circumnavigation of the world on his boat *Firecrest*. In the many books he penned, one quote stands out in explaining what attracted him to the sea:

'I wanted freedom, open air and adventure. I found it on the sea.'

Such an apt sentiment to sum up the life of Alain Gerbault!

Alain as a First World War pilot

Alain Gerbault on his arrival in Le Havre in 1929

Alain standing on the Firecrest in New York

Alian visiting Queen Marau of Tahiti

Firecrest in Morocco

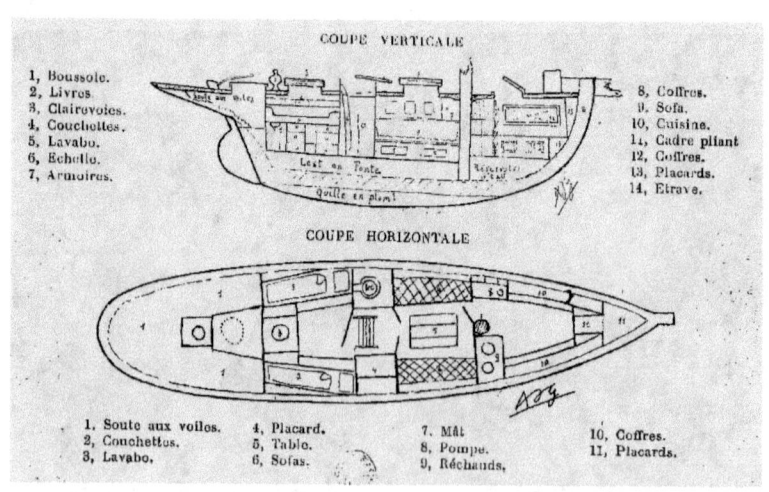

The interior layout of Firecrest

Chapter 19

Norbert Casteret

Norbert Casteret

...exploring alone is my favourite occupation, the most exciting thing I know. It demands absolute self-reliance.

Norbert Casteret was a prolific cave explorer from the Pyrenees Mountains during the first half of the last century. He discovered extensive new cave systems, a number of which contained evidence of prehistoric use. Many of his explorations were carried out alone using the rudimentary equipment of the day, which required tremendous physical skill and daring.

In total he discovered and explored around 2000 caves. His exploits within the underground world did a great deal for the sport of caving as well as increasing our understanding of prehistory, zoology, geology and hydrology. Many believe his feats of exploration made him one of the greatest adventurers of the twentieth century.

Early life

Norbert was born in 1897 in the village of Saint Martory in the foothills of the Pyrenees in France. His was quite an affluent family – his father was a lawyer. Norbert first began visiting caves when he was five, when his family took him into the nearby Bacuran Cave. By the age of eleven he had been into most of the accessible caves in the region, some of which he visited on his own.

By the time he was a teenager he had turned into a talented all-round sportsperson, proficient in soccer, swimming, diving, skiing, boxing, rowing, cycling, pole vaulting, gymnastics and mountaineering. He was awarded the Champion of the Pyrenees running medal and was the Pyrenees ski-jumping champion for one winter season.

However, it was the underground world that really fascinated him. He once wrote:

The cool air, the damp soil, and soundless blackness made a striking contrast with the world outside. They created an atmosphere of their own. I was entering another, a mysterious world, which scared me at the same time, it filled me with mystical enthusiasm.

His fascination with the subterranean world grew as he visited more caves. Having developed an array of physical skills no doubt helped him journey through narrow passageways, scale underground waterfalls, climb down shafts and dive into flooded subterranean streams. At the age of fifteen, on his own, he visited the Poudac-Gran Cave where he used a rope to descend a 35 metre shaft. With candles to light his way, he eventually discovered a large chamber, a lake and the remains of bear bones.

In World War One, he volunteered for the French Infantry. During his three years of service he fought in the trenches but luckily was not injured. When the war ended Norbert kept hold of his helmet and lamp so he could use them on caving trips. Deciding on a career, he initially trained as a notarial lawyer but, after a period of time, abandoned this in order to study geology and archaeology.

His early subterranean discoveries

Norbert spent much of his time roaming the high slopes of the Pyrenees Mountains looking for holes in the ground where there might be a new cave to explore. With the region having numerous areas of limestone, it was an ideal place in which to discover new caves. If he happened to come across an unknown one, he ventured inside using candles to light his way. If he came upon a shaft in the dark, he would throw stones down or drop burning paper to estimate its depth. He once wrote:

...exploring alone is my favourite occupation, the most exciting thing I know. It demands absolute self-reliance.

In 1923 he struck lucky. In an attempt to travel further as he explored the Montespan Cave, he free-dived a flooded passageway some 60 metres inside the cave!

He calculated that beyond the submerged passageway he should emerge into air. Taking off his clothing in case it got caught on rocks, he plunged into total darkness. The water was exceedingly cold as he held his breath and felt his way through the restricted space. All he took with him were some matches and candles in a waterproof bag in order to explore beyond the flooded section. This is believed to be the first time such a daring subterranean dive had been attempted. His hunch proved correct because he emerged into a passageway with air.

During return trips to the Montespan Cave he discovered 1.5 kilometres of new cave and found prehistoric statues and other artwork from a time when early humans had used the cave for shelter. Norbert made prehistoric discoveries in other caves during this period: bear skeletons, and etchings of hyenas, mammoths and bison from a period when the region had a different climate.

In 1924 Norbert married Elisabeth, a keen mountaineer; she also developed a passion for cave exploration and became one of the world's first women cave explorers.

In 1926 Norbert, Elisabeth, his mother and brother explored Grotte Casteret (which was named after him) whose entrance was 2743 metres up on the upper reaches of a mountain. Being so high, the cave contained a frozen lake and numerous ice features that had slowly built up over time. On a different outing in 1928, Norbert and Elisabeth found human remains from the Roman period in a cave called Girosp.

In the same year, Norbert began a prolonged search for the source of the River Garonne, a huge undertaking that involved a great deal of investigation. The mystery was finally solved three years later when he threw 60 kilos of fluorescent dye into the subterranean water system. The coloured water travelled four kilometres inside the mountain and thus established the exact course of the underground river.

His action eventually stopped the development of a hydro-electric scheme by the Spanish. Norbert had proved that the planned diversion of the river would deprive people of water on the French side of the mountain. Around the same time, he discovered prehistoric engravings of horses, human masks, bison and lion heads in the Baronies Cave. In a different cave system, he discovered pictures of stars, sun wheels and other astrological symbols dating as far back as the Iron Age.

Norbert continually looked out for unexplored caves:

One winter evening I was returning from a ski ascent of the Pic de Cagire...The sun had just set as I coasted down the last slopes...my eye fell on a group of trees around a circular depression...I went over out of curiosity.

After throwing down snowballs to ascertain its depth, he realised he had discovered yet another new cave. During return visits he eventually explored the extensive Grotte de Cagire.

<u>An expert of the underworld</u>

Norbert became well known for his underground adventures and his knowledge of the subterranean world, and he was often called upon to advise on the construction of hydro-electric schemes proposed by France and Spain on both sides of the Pyrenees. During his research for such projects he discovered the extensive Cigalière Cave system.

This challenging cave was difficult to explore because of the numerous underground waterfalls that he needed to climb up. However, his exploration led him to one impressive passageway that was full of rare, delicate crystal formations. Also during this period he explored Gouffre Martel which, at that time, was the deepest cave in France.

In 1934 Norbert and Elisabeth were invited by the Moroccan authorities to explore caves and establish an underground water supply that could be utilised by the city of Taza. They worked non-stop for 45 days, travelling deep underground through passageways, chambers and shafts.

Returning to the Pyrenees, Norbert began a three-year research project to study the bat population in his local caves. During the project he was involved in ringing more than 5000 bats to track their flight; indeed, he became an expert naturalist on the wildlife of caves.

With his knowledge of the subterranean world, he gave lectures about cave-related topics in many countries and also wrote about his exploits: during his lifetime he wrote more than 500 articles and 45 books, many of which were translated into different languages. His talks and writing encouraged many more people to take up the sport of caving.

Later years

Elisabeth died in 1940, not long after giving birth to their fifth child. During World War Two Norbert arranged for 15 tons of arms and ammunition, together with secret documents, to be hoarded in different caves; the munitions were used by the French Resistance. In 1947 he received the Legion of Honour for the part he had played during the war.

That same year, Norbert explored the Henne-Morte Cave where he and friends spent a week caving and camping underground, a practice that was unheard of at the time. During this period he also began serious caving trips with two of his children, Maud and Gilberte. They discovered new caves full of ice features high up in the mountains of the Gavarnie region of the Pyrenees. On another of their family journeys, one of his daughters developed appendicitis while she was underground.

In 1951 Norbert spent time exploring another extensive cave, the Pierre St Martin, with fellow caving friends; at that time, it held the record as being the deepest cave in the world. Unfortunately a close friend, Marcel Loubens, died on one of their trips into the cave and it was difficult to retrieve the body because of the extreme underground terrain. With Norbert at the centre of the rescue project, it took two years to work out a way of extricating Marcel's body back to the surface.

Norbert, with fellow speleologists, continued exploring the Cigalière Cave system in 1955 and found yet more new passageways. In total, they had to climb 52 challenging waterfalls before they finally reached the end of the cave; it had taken him thirty-three years of on-and-off exploration to find its end.

Norbert remained physically active in later life, which allowed him to continue visiting the subterranean world albeit into less demanding caves. At the age of 73 he could still perform somersaults, much to the amusement of his family and friends. He died in 1987 aged 90.

A commemorative stamp of Norman Casteret

*Elisabeth and Norbert standing with caving tackle
(Credit: Gilberte Casteret)*

Elisabeth and Norbert

Norbert Casteret wrote many books and articles about caving. (Credit: Gilberte Casteret)

*Norbert free-diving in a cave system
(Credit: Gilberte Casteret)*

Norbert in a narrow passageway (Credit: Gilberte Casteret)

Norbert was always searching for new caves on the slopes of the Pyrenees Mountains (Credit: Gilberte Casteret)

Chapter 20

Plennie Wingo

Plennie Wingo

...he decided he would walk backwards around the world! If successful, he believed his stunt would achieve both fame and fortune.

Plennie Wingo holds the distance record for walking backwards. He completed this unusual feat during the 1930s by reverse walking almost 13,000 kilometres across the United States and Europe.

Earlier life

Plennie was born in Texas in the USA in 1895. His father died when he was only a baby; his mother went on to marry his father's younger brother and, in time, had a total of ten brothers and sisters.

From a very early age Plennie was an enterprising boy. To make a few cents pocket money he would catch rattlesnakes using a stick then sell them to people either as food or for their skins. In school he worked reasonably hard but he was often restless, dreaming about how he could become rich. As a teenager, when he was not in school he waited tables in his hometown of Abilene.

Plennie married Idella Richards in 1915 and not long afterwards they had a daughter they named Vivian. In 1924 he successfully opened a cafe and the family prospered. These were boom years in the USA when businesses were springing up across the nation, and wealth and optimism were in the ascent. However, it was also during prohibition and the authorities caught Plennie selling alcohol on his premises; he was duly handed a hefty fine.

In 1929 the Great Depression affected the entire world. Like many others, Plennie was unable to continue with his business and was declared bankrupt.

Across the United States

Americans were in shock – how were they going to make a living, feed their families and simply survive? However, a few creative thinkers came up with novel ideas to make some money; one man, Alvin Kelly, decided to sit on top of a flagpole for 49 days! Then there was Bill Williams, who pushed a peanut up Colorado's Pikes Peak in 1929 using only his nose! The mountain stood at 4,302 metres and it took him 21 days. These, together with other equally bizarre ideas, were all schemes to make money through sponsorship or bets. Entrepreneurial

Plennie came up with his own plan: after considerable thought, he decided he would walk backwards around the world! If he was successful, he believed his stunt would give him both fame and fortune.

Plennie calculated his backward journey would take about three years to complete and began his preparations. He asked a doctor for advice who gave him tips on strengthening certain muscles. Plennie practised walking backwards each day and experimented with using a mirror at arm's length to help him avoid obstacles to his rear, but he found walking in reverse was difficult and slow. How on earth could he do this all the way around the planet?

Fortunately he came across a magazine advert displaying some newly invented goggles with rear-view mirrors sticking out at the sides. These made the process much easier and he could move backwards at a far greater speed.

He was ready to begin his trek. In April 1931 Plennie Wingo, aged 35, started his journey walking backward around the world from Fort Worth in Texas. Wearing black shoes, a smart suit, necktie, a hat, his 'special glasses' and holding a walking cane, he walked backwards towards Dallas. Even though he had been practising, he found the first few days exhausting.

When he eventually reached Dallas, Plennie went straight to a city building to obtain an official stamp. He decided to carry a notebook to produce at each major location, in which he could receive an official endorsement as proof of his visit. While in Dallas, Plennie had some 25-cents postcards printed, which he intended to sell during his journey to earn some money. Each postcard had a picture of him on the front.

After Dallas he entered countryside that had been savaged by decades of overgrazing resulting in scorched fields and undernourished cattle. Each night, Plennie found a cheap hotel or would be invited into people's homes for a meal and to rest.

Plennie walked backwards through Oklahoma, where he sold many postcards. Even though the country was suffering from both dust storms and the consequences of the financial crash, people were generally very friendly. An exception was one day when he was set upon by four characters who were obviously after his cash, but fortunately a man passing in a car came to his rescue.

People were often waiting for Plennie when he entered a new town; they wanted to see this man after reading about him in the newspapers. He wasn't easy to miss because he had a sign made for his back: *WALKING BACKWARDS AROUND THE WORLD*. Occasionally, he stopped for a day and advertised a local business using a sandwich-board, shuffling backwards with an advertisement for all to see. This helped to pay for overnight stops, food and incidentals.

A major problem when travelling along main highways and in urban centres was the increasing numbers of automobiles. Road accidents across the United States were on the rise, so walking backwards along such roads was definitely a dangerous business. There was also an increase in lawlessness: gangs, prohibition, unemployment and poverty all added to the general unease. Plennie had to watch out for the police, who regularly questioned him about his unusual trip and were, on the whole, quite antagonistic towards him.

As he walked across Missouri and into Illinois, he sometimes covered 32 kilometres in a day. He sent his luggage ahead by bus to his next destination so he didn't have to carry any bulky items. One thing he did regularly, however, was to continually re-sole his shoes.

Reaching Chicago, he decided to stay with his aunt and rest. After a few days he continued his journey eastwards but tragedy struck in the town of Robertsville, Ohio, when Plennie stepped backwards straight into a hole in the road. There was a crunching sound, he fell over and was in pain. He had broken his ankle so spent the next three weeks in hospital.

When his ankle had healed, he carried on; it felt good to be walking backwards once more. In New York, Plennie found the city feeling the full force of the economic downfall, rife with poverty and closed businesses. Whilst staying with a friend, he enquired about finding a ship to take him to London but he was told that many vessels remained idle because of the financial crash and finding a passage might be difficult.

Plennie walked to Elizabeth in New Jersey, where he was offered some advertising work: he was asked to walk backwards around the 45 centimetre-wide outside ledge of the twelfth storey of the Hersch Tower! This he did and was promised a $43 payment which would help pay his fare to Europe. Sadly, after being swindled by the man organising the stunt there was a fist-fight and Plennie was taken to jail. When he was released, he was told to move on.

He had very little money to pay for his sea passage and continued walking backwards to Providence, Rhode Island. Reading his forwarded mail, Plennie received divorce papers from his wife, Idella, who wanted rid of her absent husband.

Finally, he arrived in Boston after walking across sixteen US states. He had almost no money, his wife was leaving him and he was struggling to get to Europe to continue his backward trek around the world, and he wondered what to do next. Then, quite unexpectedly, a shoe company offered Plennie a place working aboard a ship sailing from Boston to Hamburg in Germany.

Across Europe

Life was hard for him onboard the ship; he suffered terribly from sea sickness and was continually bullied by his boss who didn't exactly applaud Plennie's desire to walk backwards around the planet.

After he had worked long shifts for many days, the ship eventually reached Hamburg. With a mixture of relief and trepidation, Plennie walked backwards down the gangplank. He was immediately asked to prove to the German authorities that he was capable of walking in reverse but he demonstrated this easily to port officials in a room full of obstacles.

One of the first tasks he undertook was to have his sign changed on his back to read: *RÜCKWÄRTS Rund um die WELT*.

Plennie had been warned that Germany was being hit hard by the worldwide financial collapse. Unemployment and poverty were fuelling a countrywide crisis, and Nazi ideology was on the rise, but as he walked backwards to Berlin he stayed overnight in farm houses along the way. Helped by a German newspaper cutting from Hamburg, which explained his unusual journey, he received nothing but kindness.

After two weeks he reached Berlin where he was the subject of a Paramount newsreel movie that filmed him walking backwards at various famous sights around the city. On his way to Dresden he suffered greatly when walking backwards through the snow: it was difficult to see clearly what he was walking upon and took him much more time. On one overnight stop, the locals felt so sorry for this cold and bedraggled traveller that they kitted him out with a warmer set of clothing.

After he crossed the Czechoslovakian border, people appeared to be much less friendly; it was obvious that something about Plennie upset the bystanders. A local man pointed out that the onlookers assumed he was German after reading his sign; in this country there was an intense dislike of Germany – so he had his sign re-written in Czech.

He continued his journey to Prague, Vienna and then to Budapest. Near a river close to Sebes in Romania, he dropped the cane he had been walking with since he had started out. It fell into the river and took several dives for him to recover from the murky water.

In Bucharest a large crowd followed him around the city centre as he walked backwards trying to find a cheap hotel. In

Sofia, Bulgaria, he was briefly arrested by the police before the US Consulate intervened.

After that, Plennie shuffled backwards into Greece along very quiet, dusty roads. He was forced to sleep out under the stars one night and narrowly missed being attacked by a large snake. At the Turkish border, he was thrown into jail once again before being released, and when he eventually arrived in the outskirts of Istanbul, he saw a number of Turkish police officers coming towards him in his wing-mirrors!

Once again he was arrested and taken to jail, where he remained for many days until he was finally released into the care of the American Embassy. His arrest made international headlines: *Turkish Police Arrest Backward Walking Texan,* announced the *Baltimore Sun.*

Arriving at the gateway to Asia, it became apparent he could go no further; both the officials at the US Embassy and the Turkish authorities refused to sanction Plennie's request to travel further east. He was told:

'*You have walked through the walkable countries...A man entering [lands further to the east] would be doomed...impossible for him to survive.*'

His plan to walk backwards around the entire world had come to an abrupt end.

Finishing his journey

Initially, this refusal came as a complete shock. What was he to do? After a great deal of thought, he decided to amend his original plan; instead of walking around the world, he would return to the United States and head for California, from where he would walk backwards and return to Texas. At least he would still be the first person to walk in reverse across the North American continent as well as across Europe!

He stayed in Istanbul for several weeks, meeting people and seeing the sights. A wealthy Italian businessman offered to pay Plennie to accompany him to Marseille in France as long as he helped him transport some items to that country, and from France he obtained a passage aboard a ship back to the United States.

After sailing into New York, Plennie had more good fortune and was able to hitchhike with a man who was driving to Los Angeles. Once in California, he prepared to complete his journey.

From Los Angeles he followed the Pacific coast road to San Diego then on into Arizona. Plennie found it extremely hot in the desert where temperatures sometimes reached more than 45 degrees Celsius. He ended up in a jail in Phoenix, this time for simply walking backwards through the city. Further on he was forced to spend the night in a phone booth because he was surrounded by a pack of coyotes.

Eventually, he returned to Fort Worth, Texas, where he had started his journey. It was October 1932 and his reverse walk had taken eighteen months to complete approximately 13,000 kilometres through nine countries on two continents. He had been in jail many times, completely worn out 12 pairs of shoes and had lost weight, but he was very much fitter.

The adventure didn't earn him the fortune he had hoped for: he finished with just $4 in his pocket! As he walked backwards into Fort Worth, many of his friends and family were there to greet him, including Idella and Vivian.

Later life

Plennie returned to work as a cook and eventually Vivian joined him in the cafe where he was employed. After a period of time, Plennie and Idella re-married and opened a cafe of their own but their marriage didn't last long and they divorced again. Later he married Juanita Billingsley and both found employment in the hospitality business.

Throughout his backward walking adventure, Plennie had sworn that he would write a book about his journey. It took a long time but in 1966 Plennie finally finished *Around The World Backwards*.

In 1976, to celebrate the bicentenary of the United States, Plennie once again took to walking backwards, this time from San Francisco to Santa Monica, around 650 kilometres. He was then 81 years of age!

As time has moved on, his name and his remarkable 1930s journey have largely been forgotten. Sadly, Plennie missed out on both fame and fortune and lived his final years in obscurity; he died in Texas in 1993, aged 98. However, in 2015 his extraordinary achievement was finally recognised when Plennie Wingo was proclaimed by Guinness World Records as the record holder for the *'greatest extent of reverse pedestrianism'*. Worthwhile acclaim at last for a very deserving, determined and unusual adventurer.

Backward walking by motor cars

Plennie Wingo's glasses allowing him to see behind as he walked backwards

Plennie walking backwards out in the countryside

*Plennie Wingo with a caption from the
Chicago Tribune in 1932*

Plennie with his wife Della and daughter Vivian

Plennie's postcard explaining his trip

Chapter 21

Oskar Speck

Oskar Speck

I wanted much more to make a kayak voyage that would go down in history.

Oskar Speck travelled in a collapsible kayak all the way from Germany to Australia in the 1930s. During his seven-year-and-four-month adventure, he met with numerous dangerous situations from both the rivers and seas – and from some of the people he met along the way.

Early life

Oskar Speck was born in 1907 near Hamburg in the north of Germany. He was one of seven children from a family with limited means. His father was a harsh man who was very strict with his offspring. At the age of fourteen Oskar left school and found employment hauling heavy bags of wood chips to various locations and delivering manure by cart to nearby farms. His teenage years involved hard work but were quite uneventful.

He found relief from this mundane existence by taking up kayaking. The sport was spreading through northern Europe during the 1920s and was particularly popular in Germany, where lots of people were regularly taking to the nation's rivers and lakes. Cheap collapsible kayaks with a rubberised canvas skin stretched over a skeleton of wooden ribs, known as *faltboot,* were all the rage. Oskar started participating in the sport and became active in a local kayaking club.

By his mid-twenties he had found more challenging employment running a small electrical contracting company, but in 1929 the Great Depression took hold and hit Germany hard; 30% of the country's workers became unemployed. After Oskar's company went bankrupt, he found himself – and 21 of his fellow workers – without a job.

Paddling to Cyprus to find work

Oskar came up with a somewhat unusual and bold plan to find employment: he decided he would go to Cyprus, where he had heard miners were needed to work in the copper mines. As he could not travel by any other method, he decided he would paddle there! He ignored the warnings about the risks that might be involved and the fact that he had no money for the journey. He also ignored the fact that he couldn't swim!

The times in Germany were very catastrophic...all I wanted was to get out of Germany for a while.

In May 1932, at the age of 25, Oskar caught a train to the German town of Ulm on the River Danube where he launched his five-year-old folding kayak. This 5.5 metre two-person kayak had been modified for a single paddler. Oskar placed clothes, equipment and supplies inside his craft, as well as a camera, a pistol, sailing charts and a compass.

Heading in an easterly direction, Oskar followed the Danube through Germany then into Austria, Hungary and Romania. The tranquil Danube made his journey a little too tame so, when he reached the Vardar River near the Yugoslavian border, he switched rivers and went into Macedonia. This river had never been navigated by kayak before and was far more challenging. When he met a particularly fast-flowing stretch of water with numerous rapids, he started a wild 60 kilometre journey that badly damaged his kayak and broke half of its ribs. Without money to pay for repairs, and with the Vardar freezing over for the winter, he was forced to call a halt to his travels and find temporary work to pay for the repairs and to feed himself.

As soon as he could, Oskar continued down the Vardar River and into the Aegean Sea. He now had to learn how to travel amid swell and large waves, which wasn't straightforward in his collapsible kayak. He discovered that its foot-controlled rudder became more important than the paddle, but having never experienced sea kayaking before he continually feared capsizing. His fears were well-founded: after starting this sea leg of his journey, he experienced a near collision with an ocean freighter!

In an attempt to travel faster, Oskar modified his kayak by adding a 4.2 metre sail that doubled the vessel's speed; he also added splash-guards to keep out the water. He gradually made his way through the Mediterranean Sea by island-hopping along the Greek islands and then sticking close to the Turkish coast. He always aimed to sleep on the shore at night, believed it would be suicidal to fall asleep in his craft at sea and that it was to his advantage to stay alert.

He eventually made his way to Cyprus.

Continuing to Australia

As Oskar's journey had unfolded, he realised that he was enjoying travelling long distances in his kayak. He loved the adventure and decided that he would rather continue his trip than toil away in a copper mine, so in Cyprus he didn't even bother looking for any work but made plans to carry on paddling:

I wanted much more to make a kayak voyage that would go down in history.

He decided to continue in his little boat – all the way to Australia.

After being forbidden to travel through the Suez Canal, he headed east. Cyprus to Syria involved a long open-sea crossing and another near miss by a ship, but he eventually arrived after a 48-hour non-stop journey.

Oskar aimed for the Euphrates River, which required an overland journey by bus across a roadless desert. Paddling along the Euphrates was extremely testing because of the intense heat as well as a lack of available food and water, but he managed to survive by gathering and eating riverside dates. Unfortunately, as he paddled the Euphrates he was also regularly shot at by the local inhabitants! Further along the river he encountered a ferocious storm that resulted in him being stranded on a tiny river island for a week in the company of a decaying corpse!

When Oskar reached the Persian Gulf, he continued his journey by keeping close to the northern coast as far as Bandar Abbas on the Strait of Hormuz. There he stayed for six months as he waited for the arrival of another kayak. The German manufacturers of his vessel, Pionier Faltbootwert, had agreed to send him replacement kayaks throughout his journey believing that his adventurous undertaking would be extremely good advertising for them. Whilst he waited he contracted malaria, which plagued him for the remainder of his journey, but the pause gave his fatigued body time to recuperate. In September 1934 he moved eastwards into the Arabian Sea.

He didn't really enjoy the journey along the Persian Coast, finding it devoid of interest. To amuse himself as he paddled along he took to chasing sharks.

Often I paddled through them with no more than three metres distance between them and me, to try to get a photo...

While he slept one night at the Persian border, Oskar's kayak and possessions were stolen. He eventually found his boat tied up on the deck of a local dhow ship and was obliged to pay the crew the equivalent of £40 for its return. They insisted they had found the vessel drifting in the water!

Eventually Oskar arrived on the coast of Baluchistan (in present-day Pakistan) at the far western extent of British India. As he travelled along the coast his fame went before him; when he stopped at various ports he was regularly taken in and entertained by everyone from maharajas to the colonial community. In return, Oskar provided them with tales from his journey. His modest celebrity status also helped provide donations of much-needed cash for his trip.

There was a huge contrast between his life in these urban centres and his time out at sea. Oskar, who had by now taken to wearing a white pith helmet and khaki shorts, regularly met with the most challenging conditions in his kayak; he was continually bombarded by wild seas and monstrous waves, and experienced a number of serious capsizes. In one encounter he lost all his supplies and in another his mast snapped.

As he carried out his kayak adventure, the rise of Nazi Germany had been taking place back in his homeland. As well as being a novelty among the colonials in British India, there were rumours that Oskar was a German spy making secret maps, and that his vessel could turn itself into a diving machine and could even fly! In one port he was arrested by the authorities before being released two days later.

Oskar finally reached Colombo in Ceylon (Sri Lanka) where he decided to stay for three months to sit out the monsoon season and plan the rest of his journey.

He picked up another replacement kayak in Madras (Chennai) before travelling along the north-east Indian coast and arriving in Calcutta (Kolkata) in January 1936. By April of that year he was kayaking along the Burmese coast, once again in deadly monsoon conditions. He wrote in his journal:

It's an act of sheer madness to be travelling in a collapsible boat at this time of year. But what am I to do?

He was sometimes driven off course, and there were other occasions when he spent 30 or 40 hours gripping his paddle. When he eventually stopped, his fingers had seized up and wouldn't open.

After replacing his kayak once again, he left Singapore, crossed the Equator and headed for Butavia (Jakarta). In these waters he found it challenging when communicating to islanders because he couldn't speak their languages. There were also some of the most precarious currents and tidal flows he had met so far on his journey.

In Butavia, Oskar was befriended by the group leader of the German expatriate community and members of the Nazis Party. He was treated as a hero and given cash gifts to cover the rest of his journey; he was also provided with a Nazi pennant to fly from his kayak. He enjoyed the injection of extra funds but had little interest in the new German politics.

As he continued paddling east, his progress was slow. He again met unfavourable seas, more storms and was blown of course. He was often totally exhausted, sunburned, thirsty and unable to find food, and on a couple of occasions he had to stop his journey – once because the malaria returned.

There were other times when the usually welcoming local people became decidedly unfriendly, probably due to Oskar's inability to communicate with them. One night, as he slept on the island of Lakor in the Dutch East Indies (now Indonesia), he almost lost his life. Twenty local islanders beat him severely, leaving him semi-conscious and with a punctured eardrum. His kayak was ransacked and he'd been tied up. Luckily he managed to chew through his restraints and escape in his kayak, but he couldn't find medical help in the local villages so had to return to the Javanese city of Surabaya many hundreds of kilometres away. It took him a whole year to recover from the attack.

Such a vicious assault could well have ended Oskar's kayaking but he had become such a hardened traveller that he was determined to achieve his goal of reaching Australia. The Dutch East Indies authorities were reluctant to allow him to continue his journey along the more straightforward south coast route of New Guinea and would only allow him to travel the much longer route around the north of the island.

From the Kai Islands in the Banda Sea to Dutch New Guinea was Oskar's longest sea crossing of some 200 kilometres. He was then faced with a journey along the northern coast via Manakwari, Lae and Samarai, and eventually reached Port Moresby by August 1939. New Guinea was a tropical environment with torrential daily downpours and crocodile infested mangrove swamps, not the easiest of locations for a lone traveller in a collapsible kayak!

Having paddled through an entire night, Oskar finally reached Saibai Island in Australia's Torres Strait in early September. A small group of locals gathered to greet him, including three policemen. A report in the *Australian Post* of the time described the meeting:

'Well done, feller! You've made it – Germany to Australia in that (pointing to his kayak). But now we've got a piece of bad news for you. You are an enemy alien. We are going to intern you,' one of the officers informed Oskar.

<u>After his journey</u>

After seven years and four months, Oskar had succeeded in paddling his collapsible kayak from Germany to Australia, but due to the volatile situation where Germany and Australia had just declared war on each other, he was imprisoned as an 'enemy foreigner'. He spent the following six years in Australian internment camps, during which time he managed to escape for a number of weeks before being recaptured. He was a constant problem to the prison authorities.

Unfortunately, amid the turmoil of those wartime years, his remarkable adventure was largely forgotten.

In January 1946 Oskar was released as a prisoner of war and within four days he arrived at some opal mines near Melbourne. He became a successful opal dealer, an Australian citizen, and built a home on the Pacific coast close to Sydney where, for the last thirty years of his life, he lived with his partner, Nancy Steele. He passed away in 1995 aged 88.

Oskar Speck had completed one of the most daring voyages ever undertaken in the history of kayaking. His extraordinary journey of 50,000 kilometres has to be one of the most awe-inspiring adventures of the twentieth century.

Oskar in his kayak (Credit: Boating New Zealand)

*Oskar meeting the locals in Papua New Guinea
(Credit: Dirk Deklein)*

Oskar standing by his collapsible kayak (Credit: Dirk Deklein)

Chapter 22

Freddy Spencer Chapman

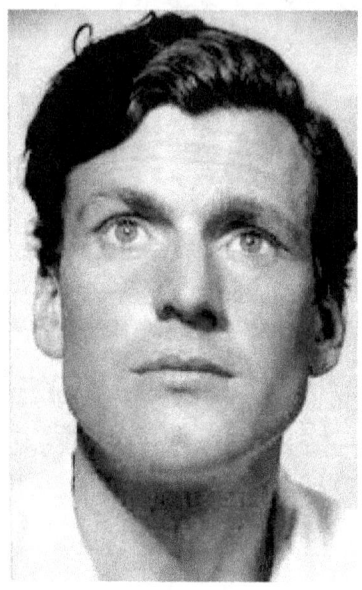

Freddy Spencer Chapman

Mere cold is a friend, not an enemy. The weather always gets better if you wait long enough; man can exist for a very long time on very little food; the human body is capable of bearing immense privation; it is the state of mind that is important.

Freddy Spencer Chapman was a British adventurer during the middle part of the last century. He became an expert on living in the Arctic, and was a mountaineer as well as being a downhill ski racer and fell runner. He was also a World War Two hero as a commando.

Freddy's lifelong passion was the natural world, and he became an expert on both bird and plant life.

Early years

Freddy was born in 1907. His parents both died when he was a young child and, as a consequence, he was brought up by clergy in two different locations on the edge of the Lake District. He spent a lot of his childhood alone exploring his surroundings and developing a love for the great outdoors and the natural world. He was an enthusiastic butterfly collector, learned to name wildflowers and became a keen bird watcher.

Freddy was sent to a boarding school on the Yorkshire Moors when he was eight years old. Fortunately for him, he was encouraged to develop his love of nature as the headteacher was also an enthusiast.

At the age of 14 he went to Sedbergh School in Yorkshire. He disliked the formal structure of school life and regularly broke the rules. He grew increasingly tough as he grew older and would ask fellow pupils to hit him on the head with a cricket bat to see how hard he could take it!

Freddy avoided games' afternoons; he believed activities like cricket and rugby were a waste of time and was regularly punished for not taking part. Eventually the headteacher gave him permission to explore the nearby hills on his own, *'as long as you don't waste time!'* For three days each week he went onto the fells from lunchtime until 7.00pm and could average around 10 kilometres per hour as he travelled over vast swathes of countryside, exploring the flora and fauna of this upland world in all weathers.

I could forget myself in the rhythm of tired muscles, in the fascination of following a compass course over the hills in thick mist...

During holidays away from school, Freddy learned to shoot game as well as other skills for poaching, which he occasionally took part in.

Climbing in Britain and the Alps

In 1926, Freddy went to Cambridge University and joined the Cambridge Mountaineering Club. He went rock climbing in North Wales, the Lake District, Scotland and the French Alps. In the Dauphiné region, he completed the difficult traverse of the Meije at 3,984 metres with friends. As well as being impressed by the climbing experience, he was excited by the abundance of Alpine flowers on the mountainsides.

Whilst at Cambridge, Freddy also became part of the 'night climbing' scene where students went out during the depths of night to climb the college roofs, pinnacles and towers. The activity was disapproved of by the authorities, which very much added to its appeal for Freddy.

He went to Iceland during the summer of 1929 with two other students. They walked across the north of the island researching bird life and collecting plants for the British Museum, living off the land, shooting birds and catching fish. Later in the same year, Freddy returned to the Alps where he continued to hone his skiing skills by ski mountaineering, ascending peaks and skiing glaciers, and sleeping in mountain huts. He became a proficient downhill racer and took part in both the Parsenn Derby and the Arlberg Kandahar ski races.

He wrote:

I think skiing is the only sport I could ever have been really good at...an excellent sense of balance, great staying power...and, enough foolhardiness to take almost any slope.

Greenland

In 1930, Freddy was invited to join the British Arctic Air Route Expedition as the ski expert, official naturalist and surveyor. This group had been tasked to investigate the terrain in eastern Greenland that lay beneath a proposed new flight path between Europe and North America.

The new route would fly over the smallest amount of sea between the continents, but the terrain it would cross in Greenland was little known. The expedition aimed to explore the region to improve existing maps.

They established a base on the eastern coast, 180 kilometres west of Angmagssalik (now called Taslilaq) and the team members spent as much time as they could with the local Inuit people learning to use local kayaks, handle dog-sled teams and hunt. Freddy became a fluent Inuit speaker and had a relationship with a local woman named Gertrude.

For more than a year he surveyed the icy interior and coastline, taking part in long and often dangerous journeys by both sled and kayak. He suffered frostbite, fell into deep crevasses, was attacked by polar bears, survived extreme storms and was stranded on ice floes. He was once so tired that he fell asleep whilst on his sled; on another occasion he was so hungry that he resorted to eating his seal-skin boots. During other trips, he only just managed to save himself from falling into a deep crevasse by holding onto the handles of his dogsled, and he survived a 20-hour storm at sea in his kayak.

One of the most challenging inland journeys was to establish a winter meteorological base to collect additional weather data from the top of the Greenland ice cap. The base was 2,600 metres above sea level; it involved a 240 kilometre sled journey into the icy interior and took many weeks to reach.

Expedition member Augustine Courtauld volunteered to overwinter alone at this remote location for five months to collect vital meteorological data. At the end of the winter, a relief party struggled to reach him and he was stranded, rapidly running out of supplies in the most appalling conditions underneath a mass of new winter snow. In a second attempt to reach Courtauld, Freddy led a three-man rescue sled team. He constantly checked their position using a compass and sextant as they travelled for 14 hours a day for 12 days of sledding. Reaching a location where the base should have been visible, they split up and skied up and down until they glimpsed the ventilation tube sticking out of a mass of snow. Freddy's precise navigation had been successful!

The expedition returned to Britain in the autumn of 1931 and Freddy decided to challenge the recently completed record for running up 42 peaks in the Lake District, known as the 'Bob Graham Round' after the man who had succeeded in completing the route.

When he was at school in Yorkshire, Freddy had taken pride in his fell-running abilities. Now he was the first person to challenge the time of this gruelling endurance fell run that was 106 kilometres in length and had 8199 metres of ascent. He experienced navigational problems in the mist and suffered from a knee injury he had picked up in Greenland after falling into a crevasse, so he just missed out on equalling the record, completing the route in 25 hours. (Bob Graham's time had been 23 hours, 39 minutes.)

In July 1932 Freddy's expedition returned to Greenland to continue their work. He was surprised to learn that Gertrude had given birth to a baby boy, though sadly the child died a year later during a flu epidemic. The second expedition was much smaller than the first and based at a different location away from the previous Inuit settlement.

The trip was marred by the death of Gino Watkins, the leader of both Greenland expeditions, who disappeared during a solo hunting trip in his kayak. The expedition members were all devastated but decided to continue their research into Greenland's terrain and climate. They carried out more challenging excursions on land and at sea. Freddy wrote:

Mere cold is a friend, not an enemy. The weather always gets better if you wait long enough; man can exist for a very long time on very little food; the human body is capable of bearing immense privation; it is the state of mind that is important.

Such profound thoughts would stand him in good stead in the future.

Himalaya

In 1934, after his last expedition to Greenland, Freddy taught in a school in the Yorkshire Dales. During his vacation in 1935 he travelled across northern Scandinavia by reindeer sled and ski, and the following year he was invited to join a party that intended to climb the 6817 metre high Mount Simvu in Sikkim.

The mountain had its difficulties, which included a very challenging wall towards the top, and the party was stopped from reaching the summit by a huge crevasse and extreme weather conditions. Staying in Sikkim, Freddy and others climbed both The Sphinx at 6976 metres and the Fluted Peak at 6501 metres in height.

Freddy was offered the position of private secretary to a British government official working in Sikkim, Bhutan and Tibet. In addition to secretarial work, he was involved with photography and film-making; in his spare time he pressed 600 plants, collected numerous seeds and made notes on Himalayan bird life.

He was given permission to attempt the then unclimbed peak of Chomolhari at 7,326 metres on the border of Tibet and Bhutan. He described the mountain, noting:

This peak...gives a greater impression of sheer height and inaccessibility than any I know...

He completed the ascent with Sherpa Pasang in May 1937. On their way down from the summit Pasang fell, taking his partner with him, though Freddy managed to halt their fall with an ice-axe arrest. They continued downwards past their previous high camp but in worsening conditions were forced to climb back up to it in a blizzard. Once there, the tent door wouldn't close and snow accumulated inside.

The following day, after another fall as they descended, they were forced to camp again in blizzard conditions lower down the mountainside. They couldn't make warm drinks or cook food because they had lost their stove when the contents of a rucksack had fallen down the mountainside, and they suffered in the intense cold as the snow continued to fill their tent.

During the descent the following day, Freddy fell into a deep crevasse. Pasang held the rope as best he could and Freddy eventually appeared at the top of the crevasse after four hours of delicate ice climbing.

This extraordinary descent from Chomolhari has been referred to as one of the most incredible mountain survival stories of the era.

The Second World War and his later years

During World War Two, Freddy spent three-and-a-half years in Malaya as a commando deployed to create havoc behind enemy lines after the Japanese invaded Singapore and Malaya. As a saboteur, he blew up trains, bridges and other military targets. Freddy and two other soldiers caused a substantial amount of turmoil and found themselves in constant danger.

As well as experiencing hazardous fighting conditions, Freddy was almost permanently sick as he battled diseases including cerebral malaria and pneumonia, was shot twice and held prisoner twice. Despite all this, whenever he could he studied tropical bird life and collected seeds for Kew Gardens!

In 1946 Freddy married Faith Townsend and was appointed development officer for the adventure education organisation 'Outward Bound'. He started to give lectures and make broadcasts on the topic of 'living dangerously'.

Freddy, Faith and their three young sons took a caravanning journey around southern and eastern Africa; once again, it was an opportunity to study the unique flora and fauna of another region of the world. During this trip he ascended Kilimanjaro; the 27,300 kilometre journey took more than a year to complete and was sponsored by Outward Bound.

In 1956 Freddy was appointed headteacher of a school in South Africa where he introduced a local version of Outward Bound. However, he found it increasingly difficult to come to terms with the growing apartheid regime; when South Africa declared itself a republic in 1961, Freddy resigned from his job in protest.

On his return to Britain, his health gradually deteriorated. In 1971, aged 64, he took his own life, leaving a note for his wife saying:

I don't want you to have to nurse an invalid for the rest of your life!

Freddy Spencer Chapman had led an extremely active and adventurous life and maintained a fascination and love for all aspects of the natural world. He was an altogether extraordinary and inspirational character.

Chomolhari (Credit: Chapman Family)

Freddy leading a desperate journey in 1931 to relieve Augustine Courtauld alone and starving on the Greenland ice cap

Greenland in the 1930s

The Meiji traverse, French Alps

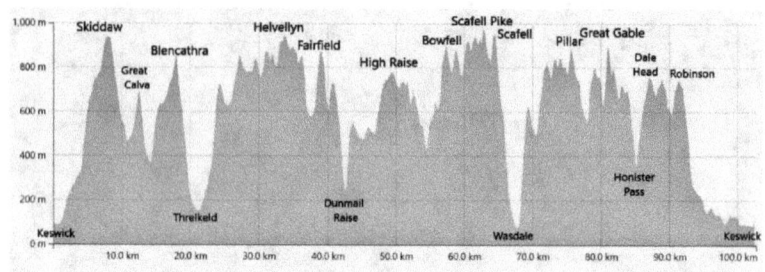

The route profile of the Bob Graham Round in the Lake District

Freddy Spencer Chapman (Credit: Chapman Family)

Chapter 23

Ang Tharkay (Credit: Dan Bryant)

Ang Tharkay

The avalanche had released one hundred metres above us...In the blink of an eye, we were caught. All three of us were knocked down and rolled over each other.

Ang Tharkay was a Sherpa who took part in numerous Himalayan expeditions during the mid-1900s. He is generally considered to be one of the most outstanding of the first generation of elite climbing Sherpas.

Early life

Ang Tharkay was born in 1907 in the village of Khunde in north-eastern Nepal. This isolated Sherpa settlement, at an altitude of around 4000 metres, is surrounded by a host of peaks. He lived with his mother, father and two younger brothers in a single-storey stone building with a wooden roof. The family had a subsistence farm on a small plot of land, growing vegetables as well as keeping goats and cows. It was a constant challenge for them to make a living. When he was old enough, Ang took charge of the family's livestock, leading them out to pasture each day upon the mountainside.

At the age of twenty-five, he moved to Darjeeling in northern India where he found employment. Arriving from his home village around the same time was a young woman called Yangjin and her family, and within months the couple had become engaged; they eventually married in Darjeeling where they made their home and raised a daughter and four sons.

Becoming a Sherpa

Ang became attracted to the idea of working in the mountains after meeting friends returning from expeditions from the Himalayas. He was captivated by their tales of climbing adventures with foreigners. He signed up as a porter with the 1931 German expedition to Kanchenjunga, but due to some confusion in the hiring process, and after trekking all the way to Base Camp, he was forced to return home.

In 1933, he went to the Himalayan Club in Darjeeling because porters were required for the British Everest Expedition in Tibet. After being deemed fit, he was hired.

Ang's first experiences as a novice porter were not the most positive because he was suffering from both flu and bronchitis. Due to his inexperience and weakness, he was bullied and mocked by the older porters but he toiled away, carrying heavy loads in freezing conditions. Remarkably, as he gained altitude and glimpsed the highest mountains, his health problems appeared to melt away. Ang felt euphoric about the environment even though he was carrying loads on his back up ever-steeper terrain.

They climbed from Base Camp to Camp I, then to an altitude of around 6000 metres to Camp II. Ang was always in the leading group of porters even though he felt the cold when walking through the snow and had difficulty breathing due to not having acclimatised. Climbing to Camp III required wearing crampons and using an ice-axe to cut steps, then he needed to use rope ladders to reach Camp IV which, thankfully, he soon mastered.

It was around this point on their way up that they could easily see Everest's summit. Ang said: *'My heart immediately began to pound, I was so moved by this sight.'*

Establishing Camp V required an immense effort in ferocious winds, after which Ang developed frostbite and had to descend the mountainside, but he had made a definite impression as a porter and was keen to find further work.

Mountain exploration

The following year Ang was invited on a small-scale expedition to the Nanda Devi Sanctuary in northern India with Eric Shipton and Bill Tilman, who tended to treat the Sherpas more as equals than employees. The aim was to find a way into the Nanda Devi massif, an impenetrable area of high mountains; during the 1930s it had been said that it was easier to get to the North Pole than to reach the Sanctuary.

Travelling by train, truck and on foot, they eventually arrived to start their exploration and, for the first time, Ang was formally made *sirdar* (lead Sherpa). They scaled cliffs, followed rivers and entered gorges in an attempt to access the higher mountains and eventually found a way into the mountain range through the

Rishi Gorge, becoming the first people to enter this isolated region.

Where others had failed, Ang often overcame challenging barriers but unfortunately the arrival of the monsoon brought a lot of snow so further exploration was put on hold. They went to the lower elevations in the Badrinath Mountain Range, another little known area. As they surveyed this new region, they ran out of food and lived mainly off fungus and bamboo shoots. Weeks later, when the weather conditions improved, they trekked back to the Sanctuary, and Ang, Eric and Sherpa Kasang climbing the 6803 metre peak, Maiktoli.

In 1935 a reconnaissance expedition was formed to explore a route up Mount Everest from the Tibetan side of the mountain. It was led by Eric Shipman, who was planning an ascent the following year, and consisted of a small group of British climbers and some of the Sherpas who had proved themselves during the Nanda Devi expedition.

From Tibet, the party ventured onto the Rongbuk Glacier and, after establishing three camps up the mountain, they reached the North Col at 7,020 metres. With monsoon weather bringing heavy snow and the reconnaissance work largely completed, they returned to Darjeeling.

Later that year Ang was again sirdar in charge of thirty porters on an expedition led by Britain's Reginald Cooke to the 7,412 metre high Kabru North on the Nepalese-Indian border. Ang climbed to around 6,700 metres before having to descend to resume his duties as sirdar. The expedition was a success, and Reginald eventually completed a solo ascent of Kabru North.

In 1936, Ang journeyed to Everest on another British expedition. Travelling from Rongbuk in Tibet, the expedition climbed to Camps I, II then III. Before ascending to Camp IV, the climbers, including Ang, were provided with special high-altitude equipment. Once again the weather deteriorated and, after three attempts to establish Camp IV, they decided to abandon the expedition. Before leaving the region, as thanks for the way Ang had distributed their rations, the men he was in charge of presented Ang with a Sherpa scarf and a horse to use during their return journey. Unfortunately, catastrophe struck on the way back: whilst crossing a river via a rope bridge, a fellow Sherpa fell in and was swept away by the whitewater below.

During the same year Ang was in the Nanda Devi Sanctuary again on Eric Shipman's second visit to the isolated region. He climbed extensively, exploring the many peaks in this secretive group of mountains:

> *This expedition made me very happy. It was different from the others I had been on. This expedition was a vacation. We only attempted the climbs that interested us…We had as much time as we wanted to relish the marvels and grandeur of the Himalayan world.*

In 1937 Eric Shipman asked Ang to be sirdar on an expedition to the Karakoram Mountains in the eastern Himalayas to survey the glaciers and mountain terrain. From Srinagar they went to the Indus Valley and into the mountains. By the end of the five-month long expedition, they had mapped almost 5000 square kilometres of hitherto little known mountain country. Ang was amazed by these new peaks; in his opinion, K2 was more beautiful than Mount Everest!

The climbers experienced a number of potentially disastrous situations. Whilst crossing a raging river, Ang was seriously concussed after hitting his head on a rock in the strong current, and Eric fell into a deep crevasse while crossing a glacier. Ang was roped up to him and managed to haul him out. Eric was unconscious so Ang ran back to alert other members of the team to help carry him back to camp.

Ang returned to Everest for his fourth visit in 1938 on a small expedition led by Bill Tilman. As a leading climber, sirdar and cook, he was kept busy throughout the expedition. Once again, the attempt was made from Tibet via the Rongbuk Glacier. From

Base Camp, the climbers established Camps I, II, III and IV before heavy snow halted their progress. Eventually, they managed to climb up to the North Col and then to Camp VI along the north ridge, with Ang climbing to over 8,200 metres.

Fellow Sherpa Pasang Bhotia suffered a stroke and was paralysed down one side of his body. Ang decided that the only way Pasang could descend was if he was carried down 'piggy-back' style with his arms wrapped around Ang's neck. This was an exhausting task: with every step, Ang sank deeply into fresh snow because of his extra load. Crossing a gorge was a challenging manoeuvre requiring assistance from others using ropes, but eventually Ang carried his friend to safety.

The Himalayan Club awarded him the prestigious 'Tiger Medal' for his mountaineering skills at high altitude; he was one of only a few recipients to receive the award. He wrote:

We were now experienced mountain climbers. We had earned the rank of "Tiger"... Our daily salary was increased... and we were given a red patch that showed our rank...

In 1939, Ang went on his second trip to the Karakoram to survey the region for future expeditions. The visit was intended to last for sixteen months but was cut short due to the outbreak of World War II. With no expedition work available, Ang became a transport agent in Darjeeling organising ponies, cooks and porters for local treks. In 1945, he guided a few British servicemen who were on leave to the summits of Chomiomo (6828 metres) and Pauhunri (7,128 metres) in the Eastern Himalaya.

Annapurna

In 1950, Ang was sirdar for a French expedition travelling to the Annapurna Massif in Nepal led by Maurice Herzog. When he met the climbing team Ang was impressed by their kindness, athleticism and their equipment.

They eventually reached Base Camp between the two great 8000 metre peaks of Dhaulagari and Annapurna. After much reconnoitring, there was a big debate as to which of the two the expedition should climb. A local Tibetan lama gave his opinion adding (through Ang's translation) that it would be better to concentrate their efforts on Annapurna, and the decision was made.

The climbers gradually moved up the mountain to Camp V at around 7300 metres. Maurice offered Ang a place on the summit team but reluctantly he had to decline because his feet were painful with possible frostbite. Maurice Herzog and Louis Lachenal climbed the summit of Annapurna (8091 metres), the first time in history that an 8000 metre high mountain had ever been climbed, but conditions were horrendous and both men suffered from frostbite that eventually resulted in them losing fingers and toes.

With other members of the team suffering snow-blindness, descending Annapurna became a logistical nightmare. An extraordinary effort was made to transport the injured by using makeshift sleds, human baskets and stretchers, during which Ang played a crucial role. The Annapurna expedition members received huge acclaim as soon as the news broke in France, resulting in Maurice Herzog, Louis Lachenal and Ang Tharkay receiving the highest award in France: the Légion d'Honneur.

The first Sherpa to do so, Ang later wrote a book about his life entitled: *Mémoires d'un Sherpa.*

The following year, he joined the 1951 British Expedition to Mount Everest led by Eric Shipton. This was a reconnaissance trip looking for possible routes up the mountain from the Nepalese side after the Tibetan border had been closed to foreigners.

After straying into Tibetan territory Ang persuaded the armed border guards to fine the expedition members rather than put them in jail, and the climbers eventually worked out a route up the Khumbu Icefall and Western Cwm that would lead them onto the South Col. From that point, they could reach the summit.

The following year most of the climbers, including Ang, were back on what should have been an ascent of Everest but their trip had to be postponed because a Swiss attempt was taking place. They turned their attention to nearby Cho Oyu, which they attempted to climb, as well as training with newly designed high-altitude equipment.

In 1953, Ang joined a Swiss expedition that aimed to climb the 8,167 metre Dhalagiri in Nepal. Once again, he was at the forefront of the attempt, but unfortunately he fell 100 metres through a cornice high up on the mountain. He managed to cling to a rocky spur before being rescued by another member of the team; luckily he was not injured and could continue climbing.

Later that same year Ang was climbing Nun Kun in the Indian Himalaya on a French/Swiss/Indian/Sherpa expedition. After heavy snowfall, they decided to descend from Camp III at 6,400 metres because the conditions were considered too dangerous for an assault on the summit. A few hundred metres from Camp II, there was a horrible cracking sound from above and snow and ice crashed down on the climbing party, including Ang who had been leading the group on a rope of three. Ang wrote:

The avalanche had released one hundred metres above us...In the blink of an eye, we were caught. All three of us were knocked down and rolled over each other. Luckily, we had fallen into deep snow.

Ang broke several ribs but fortunately all three climbers survived.

Later years

In 1954, Ang became an instructor at the newly established Himalayan Mountaineering Institute (HMI) in Darjeeling whose purpose was to encourage mountaineering in India. In the same year, he was sirdar on the first American expedition to the Himalayas. Their aim was to ascend the unclimbed 8,485 metre Makalu in the north of Nepal. The team managed to climb to 7,100 metres before bad weather forced them to descend.

The following year Ang was part of an Indian expedition from the HMI that was making the second ascent of Kamet (7,756 metres) in northern India. The leader of the expedition was Narendra Jayal, the principal of the institute. The ascent was a success and five members, including Narendra and Ang, reached the summit.

Ang was sirdar on the very first Indian Everest Expedition of 1960, but bad weather conditions resulted in the expedition being abandoned. During the second Indian Everest Expedition in 1962 he was again sirdar – and again poor weather halted progress though Ang did manage to climb up to the South Col, becoming the oldest person (at the age of 55) to climb to 8000 metres.

With his expedition days coming to an end, Ang built a house and farm in a rural area to the south of Kathmandu, but in 1978 at the age of 70, he was coaxed out of retirement to become sirdar for the final time for the French Alpine Guide attempt on Dhaulagiri led by Jean Coudray. Unfortunately, as the summit team tackled the Southwest Buttress strong winds halted their attempt.

For many years Sherpa Ang Tharkay played a central role in numerous expeditions during the 'golden years' of Himalayan mountaineering. He was a talented high-altitude climber, recipient of the coveted Tiger Medal and a sought-after sirdar.

Those who journeyed with Ang had nothing but praise for this extraordinary mountain man. He was renowned for his resourcefulness, bravery, determination, adventurous spirit, abundant skills, modesty and sense of humour; most significantly, he could always be relied on in any crisis. Ang set a high standard for future Sherpas to emulate.

After spending his final years living peacefully on his mountain farm in Nepal, he passed away in 1981 at the age of 74.

Annapurna (Credit: Sudan Shrestha)

Hauling loads in the Rishi Ganga Gorge, Nanda Devi Sancturary (Credit: Bill Tilman)

Kanchenjunga, Ang's first expedition (Credit: Alan Gough)

Khunde village beneath Khumbia, where Ang grew up. Mount Everest, Lhotse and Ama Dablem in the background.

Mount Lhotse, Mount Everest and Mount Makalu (Credit: Alan Gough)

Maurice Herzog being carried down Annapurna by Sherpas in 1950 (Credit: Alpinismus, Munich)

Chapter 24

Walter Greaves

Walter Greaves

Here is Walter Greaves attempting to break the World Year Cycle Endurance Mileage Record. He is a vegetarian, non-drinker, non-smoker and does this for pleasure.

Walter Greaves was a one-armed British cyclist who, in 1936, broke the World Year Cycle Endurance Mileage Record when he cycled a total of 45,383 miles during the year, despite travelling through atrocious weather conditions, coming off on numerous occasions and being hospitalized. *(All measurements for this chapter are imperial as it is a 'mileage' record).*

Early life

Born in 1907, Walter Greaves was the eldest child of a family of seven. He was brought up in the industrial town of Bradford in Yorkshire. His father was a quack doctor who frequented local fairs selling herbal potions and remedies; he was also a blacksmith, but unfortunately had a regular habit of taking to drink. This contributed to Walter having a tragic accident! Whilst driving his car when drunk, his father crashed into a lamppost and Walter's arm had to be amputated below the elbow.

Fortunately, Walter was made of stern stuff and refused to let this setback curtail his life even though he was sometimes bullied due to only having one arm. A confident and positive individual, he achieved success when playing rugby, when ballroom dancing and as a sprinter.

Walter became a staunch socialist and advocated major changes to society. Having such left leanings and one arm made it hard for him to secure employment; he spent most of his twenties unemployed and with very little money.

Cycling

Walter began cycling with friends around the Yorkshire dales and moors on a bicycle made of bits and pieces discarded by others. Having placed a successful bet on a horse race, he used his earnings to purchase a lightweight racing bicycle. He also found employment and was able to buy proper cycling shoes, clips and straps, which made riding his new bike much easier. He achieved good results in distance races: 50 miles in 2 hours 20 minutes; 100 miles in 4 hours 43 minutes; and 192 miles in 12 hours!

Walter had an exceptionally strong physique. He became a vegetarian and a teetotaller, the latter decision influenced by his father's love for the drink! Whenever his cycling club members stopped at cafes to tuck into their meat sandwiches, Walter would eat raw cabbage and comment to his friends: *'Meat is second-hand vegetables.'*

One day Norrie Ward, a prominent personality within the Yorkshire cycling scene, asked quite unexpectedly: *'How many miles do you think you could ride in a year, Walter?'*

After some reflection, Walter replied: *'With good luck and no unreasonable delays, 47,000 miles.'*

This was the point when he started to consider attempting to break the world record for the greatest distance cycled in a year, which stood at 43,966 miles. Unemployed again, he certainly had time to train for the distance record, but he needed funds for his everyday life. Norrie said he would become his manager and provide Walter with £3 a week for his daily needs.

Walter decided to make an attempt on the world distance record but finding sponsorship for his challenge seemed impossible. In desperation, he cycled to Coventry where he hoped to secure a new machine but he hit bad weather; the snow and icy roads resulted in many falls.

When he eventually reached the factory, Walter managed to secure a new bicycle because the management were impressed by his efforts. His new machine arrived in Yorkshire on 28th December, leaving very little time to modify it before the start of the new year. Two brakes were added using just one lever, a three-gear system and a cup holder on the handlebar that could be used for either drinks or as a place where Walter could rest the stump of his arm.

A sealed mileometer recorded the distance Walter travelled and he was asked to obtain signed documents to witness his daily progress, as well as sending postcards from his end-point each day; he would also be subjected to 'on-the-spot' checks during his challenge.

His aim was to beat the 1933 record of Australian Ossie Nicholson. Much of the Australian's year-long journey was on smooth racing tracks with a back-up car containing a manager and mechanic. In addition, Ossie's sleeping arrangements and food were taken care of. By contrast, Walter would be on his own, riding a standard bike, finding his own lodgings, carrying out his own maintenance – and facing the full force of British weather on busy roads!

Let the record attempt begin!

On 6th January 1936, the Lord Mayor of Bradford started Walter's challenge. Aled Owen's book entitled *Walter Greaves – True Yorkshire Grit* best describes the scene:

So, almost unnoticed, a shabbily dressed, unemployed Yorkshireman of sallow complexion left Bradford on the start of an attempt to break the World Year Cycle Endurance Mileage Record.

Due to delays, he had just 360 days to complete his world record attempt.

Walter started with excursions from his home in Bradford to various Yorkshire locations and also travelled to London and back. There were times when snow and ice made cycling extremely difficult; he also experienced winds, some reported to be as high as 100 mph! During one storm, Walter narrowly missed being hit by a heavy tree branch.

Cycling through town centres was challenging in case his front wheel got caught in tram lines; travelling along trunk roads could also spell danger from the heavy lorries that passed him. Riding well to the left of busy roads he risked hitting roadside debris, but the centre of such roads came with additional dangers.

As a result, Walter took many falls; he learned that falling clear of his machine was less painful than landing on top of it!

He got into the habit of recording his journey at different occasions during each day and asked witnesses to sign a card with his photograph on it. On the 17th of January, a *Pathé News* camera crew filmed Walter cycling in snow with the commentary:

'Here is Walter Greaves attempting to break the World Year Cycle Endurance Mileage Record. He is a vegetarian, non-drinker, non-smoker and does this for pleasure.'

Walter preferred hilly to flatter terrain and enjoyed cycling over the more testing Yorkshire hills and those of mid-Wales than the easier, flatter regions like the low-lying Vale of York. By the 9th of March, he had passed the 8,000 mile mark.

Having one arm resulted in him having a unique riding style that put a lot of stress on his handlebars, a number of which he broke during his record attempt. He changed his tyres whenever they showed any signs of wear as he found it difficult to mend punctures.

By 25th April, he had ridden over 13,500 miles and told reporters: *'I do not find riding over 120 miles a day dull in the least. I am enjoying the adventure immensely.'*

To increase his protein input, Walter upped his milk intake to eight pints a day. He had started to feel tired during the longer cycling days, but he felt the benefits immediately. Walter completed rides across North Wales, Northern England and to London, and broke his daily distance record when he rode 220 miles from Chester to Croydon.

His run of good fortune came to an abrupt end. Due to a previous collision with a lorry, he had to have an abscess treated in a Bradford hospital. He was discharged after two weeks but it took time and great determination to resume his long days in the saddle.

As summer turned into autumn, the nation's press realised that Walter was on target to complete a new world endurance cycling record. Finally, on 13th December 1936, Walter rode into Hyde Park in London surrounded by hundreds of fellow cyclists. He had beaten the previous record!

At a reception held in his honour, Walter was offered some 'proper food' and champagne, to which he replied: *'When I want to poison myself, I will do it properly – with arsenic.'* He continued until the end of the month, taking his total to 45,383.7 miles for riding his bicycle in one year.

On the 31st of December, the Mayor of Bradford presented Walter with trophies, and in addition, he received cheques totalling £125 from some of his sponsors. His achievement was then formally entered into the *Guinness Book of Records*.

After his success

Walter had many engagements after his world record. In March 1937, he married a woman named Rene, and they set up home in Bradford. Unfortunately, his funds ran out after a couple of years and once again he found himself on the dole.

Through his cycling contacts, he started making his own bicycles, and when war broke out he helped build air-raid shelters. After the war, he continued making cycles and opened his own shop in Bradford. He became a skilled workman, repairing a whole range of broken items from bicycles to prams.

Walter took part in and organised cycling events across the nation. Sadly his cycle shop burned down in 1950 so he was unemployed again. He started running a cyclist's cafe and selling scrap metal. These were hard days to bear, during which time Walter and Rene's relationship soured and the couple parted.

In 1956 Walter married Margaret, a musician, and they had four children. He decided to retrain as a blacksmith. Influenced by his wife, he learned to play the concertina and wrote and performed protest songs. He appeared at numerous folk concerts and became known as *The Singing Blacksmith*. He also wrote poetry.

In 1987, aged 80, Walter Greaves died. His had been a life where determination had overcome the tragedy of losing his arm when he was young. He was not only a world-record beating cyclist but a man of many other talents, a remarkable character – indeed, a Yorkshireman of *'true grit'*.

'Yorkshire Observer 1936' recognises the 'intrepid cyclist'

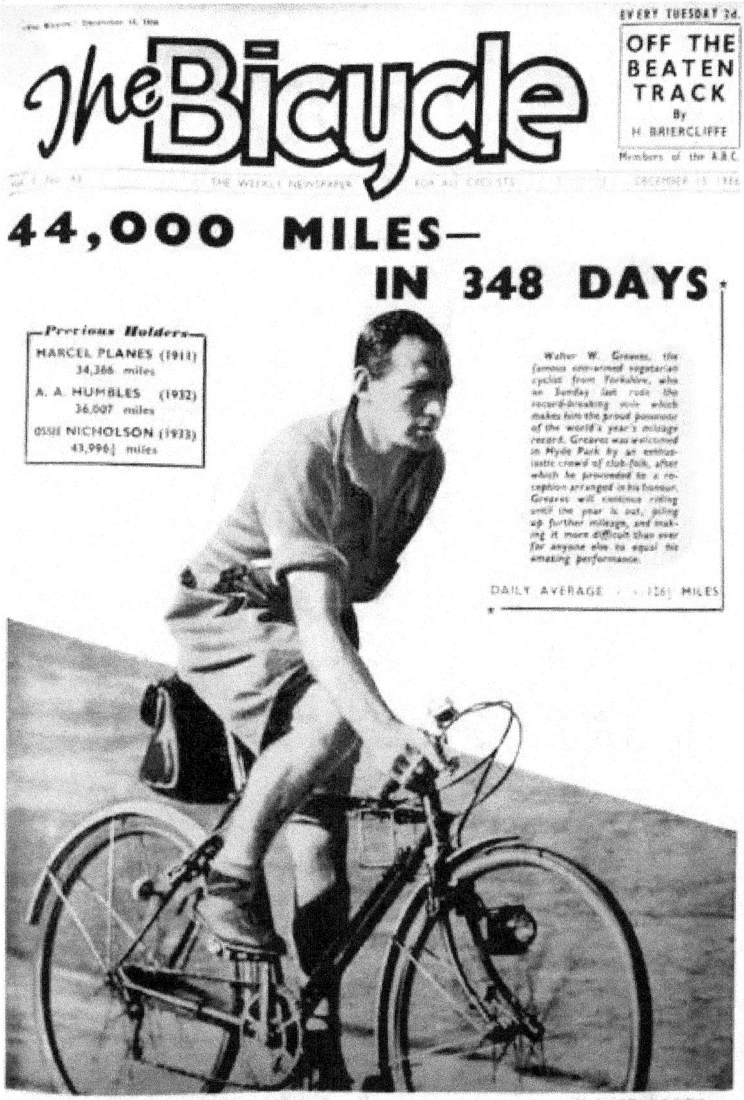

EVERY TUESDAY 2d.

The Bicycle

OFF THE BEATEN TRACK
By
H. BRIERCLIFFE

Members of the A.B.C.

THE WEEKLY NEWSPAPER FOR ALL CYCLISTS

44,000 MILES— IN 348 DAYS

Previous Holders

MARCEL PLANES (1911)
34,366 miles

A. A. HUMBLES (1932)
36,007 miles

OSSIE NICHOLSON (1933)
43,996½ miles

Walter W. Greaves, the famous one-armed vegetarian cyclist from Yorkshire, who on Sunday last rode the record-breaking mile which makes him the proud possessor of the world's year's mileage record. Greaves was welcomed in Hyde Park by an enthusiastic crowd of club-folk, after which he proceeded to a reception arranged in his honour. Greaves will continue riding until the year is out, piling up further mileage, and making it more difficult than ever for anyone else to equal his amazing performance.

DAILY AVERAGE - - 126½ MILES

Walter Greaves on his Coventry Three Spires Bicycle

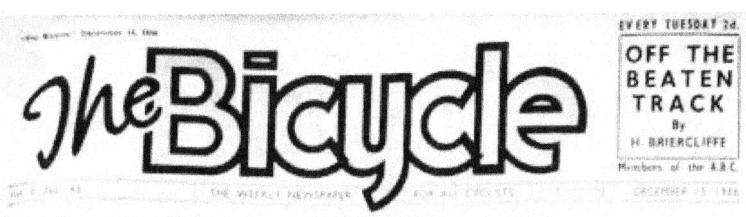

'The Bicycle' celebrates Walter Greaves!

'Three Spires' (Credit: Craven Herald and Pioneer)

Cover picture of Aled Owen's 'Walter Greaves - True Yorkshire Grit'

Chapter 25

Loulou Boulaz

Loulou Boulaz

Each one of these climbs was a first ascent by a woman climber ...many male mountaineers became irritated by such success.

Loulou Boulaz was one of the most successful female mountaineers of the 1900s. She was an extreme Swiss climber, ascending some of the hardest mountain routes in the Alps. She was also a gifted international alpine skier.

Early years

Louise Boulaz or 'Loulou' as she was generally known, was born in Avenches in Switzerland in 1908. When she was nine years of age, her family moved to Geneva. As a child, she experienced economic hardship; her father was a coach builder but was often unemployed and her mother, a former teacher, ran a cafe to make ends meet.

At school Loulou was academically successful and became fluent in a number of languages. She also possessed considerable athletic talent: she was very good at gymnastics and displayed a natural ability for skiing.

Loulou enjoyed the competitive nature of skiing and she was selected to take part in a number of downhill competitions. As her skills developed her talents were noticed by national bodies for the sport, and from 1936 until 1941 she was a member of the Swiss Ski Team. This was a remarkable achievement considering that she had a full-time job and wasn't always available for training sessions. She also became more involved with climbing, which sometimes curtailed her availability for training.

In 1937 Loulou came fourth in the World Slalom Championships in Chamonix, France, and the following year she was first in a race at Morzine in France. She stopped skiing for her country in 1941 when significant worldwide competitions were discontinued due to the Second World War.

When she left school Loulou had found employment working as a copyist for the League of Nations in Geneva, then worked as a stenographer at the International Labour Organisation (ILO) whose headquarters were in the city. Both of these posts appealed to her growing political consciousness; the ILO supported workers' rights and equal pay for women. Loulou was aware of social injustices in Swiss society at the time, particularly concerning women; women living in Switzerland didn't get the vote until 1971!

All her life Loulou protested against a range of injustices in the world whenever she could. Her friends sometimes referred to her as 'Loulou la Rouge' (Loulou the Red).

Climbing the most challenging Alpine routes

In 1932, Raymond Lambert, an aspiring Genevan guide, suggested that Loulou should try climbing. He recognised her athletic prowess, including the balance, strength and focussed mind-set required for skiing, and suggested that such attributes could easily be transferred to mountaineering.

Loulou visited the limestone cliffs of Mont Salève, just twenty kilometres from the centre of Geneva, where she served her apprenticeship on climbs of up to 180 metres. She was a natural and could tackle most of the challenges on offer.

From the top of the Salève, the sight of the Mont Blanc Massif over the border in France beckoned the climber to greater heights. Her first outing into the French massif, together with her mentor, was climbing the 3192 metre high Aiguille du Peigne. Every weekend after that through the following season Loulou and Raymond cycled ninety kilometres from Geneva to Chamonix and climbed mountains in the Mont Blanc region.

Although Loulou rapidly became an extremely competent climber, she always felt on the fringes of the local Genevan climbing scene. As a woman she didn't feel comfortable, and she also felt out of place because she was from a humbler background compared to the well-heeled men who climbed. On one occasion her principles came to the fore when she was invited to eat at one of the male climber's houses. Loulou insisted that the cook, who had spent hours preparing the food, ate at the table with them.

As Loulou's climbing developed, she tackled more and more challenging routes in the Alps. For a time she teamed up with another talented female Swiss mountaineer, Lucie 'Lulu' Durant and they became a formidable, all-female team taking on some seriously difficult mountain routes including the Dent du Géant,

Dent du Requin; the challenging and exposed climbs were a first ascent by a woman. Some male mountaineers were irritated by their success and refused to acknowledge their achievements even when, in some cases, they had actually witnessed the ascents!

Loulou's climbing ambitions expanded and she saw no reason why she shouldn't attempt some of the last unclimbed challenges within the Alps. In 1935, pairing up with Raymond Lambert again, she tackled the then unclimbed Central Spur of the North Face of the Grandes Jorasses, an intimidating undertaking; there had been five previous attempts but all had failed. They climbed for two days up the 4,208 metre mountain during which time they were exposed to a particularly intense lightning storm. On reaching the summit, they learned that a German pair had beaten them by just two days, but it was still the first ascent by a woman.

The pair went on to complete the second ever ascent of the North Face of the Petit Dru, which was also the first ascent by a woman. The 800 metre face was an extraordinary feat of climbing requiring the most advanced mountaineering skills.

By completing these north faces, Loulou gained further notoriety. Many other challenging routes followed including different climbs on the Brenva Face of Mont Blanc, the North Face of the Aiguille Noire de Peuterey and the East Face of Bec D'Oiseau (a first ascent by any person).

As World War Two unfolded, climbing in the Mont Blanc area stopped when the border was closed into France so Loulou journeyed to the Valais and Bernese Oberland regions of Switzerland and climbed with Pierre Bonnant, a partnership which friends described as being 'beyond just mountaineering'. They completed dozens of challenging new climbs, many with north faces or with exposed and technical ridges, many of which were first ever ascents, or first ascents by a woman. They included the north faces of the Schreckhorn and the Studerhorn which were both first female ascents. They also completed the most challenging of the ridges on the Matterhorn, the Furggen

Ridge. Probably the most notable climb during this period was an ascent of the North Face of the Zinalrothorn in 1941, a first ascent by any person; they climbed the 800 metre face in just five hours!

When the war was over Loulou and Pierre returned to the Mont Blanc region, which they both preferred. Their achievements included winter climbs on the Grépon and Aiguille de Bionnassay and a successful ascent of the North Face of the Aiguille Verte.

In 1952, Loulou completed the first female ascent of the Walker Spur on the Grandes Jorasses. This particular climb was a life-changing experience for both Loulou and Pierre; due to extreme weather conditions, which included heavy snowfall as well as dangerous falling rocks. They were forced to bivouac for three nights high up on the mountain. Both developed frostbite; Pierre had to have both feet amputated and Loulou lost two toes. It was the end of Pierre's climbing career.

Loulou was completely devastated by the event, so distraught that she destroyed all her climbing diaries that she had been keeping over the years. Afterwards Pierre took to sailing but Loulou continued to climb and ski; both as she explained were 'essential to her life'.

Her later years

In 1959, Loulou joined an all-female expedition to the 8181 metre Cho Oyo in the Himalayas with twelve climbers from five different nations. Loulou had problems acclimatising and was recovering away from the mountain when tragedy struck: an avalanche high on the mountain resulted in four members of the expedition being killed.

Returning to the Alps, Loulou continued climbing difficult routes including the steep wall on the North Face of the Cima Grande di Lavaredo in the Dolomite Alps in Italy, another first ascent by a woman. This climb required the ascent of a 300 metre high vertical, overhanging cliff. She also climbed Piz Badile, another one of the great north faces of the Alps on the border between Italy and Switzerland.

In 1962 Loulou made her final attempt to climb the North Face of the Eiger, a route she had previously tried to climb three times without success. Once again, this elusive and hugely challenging route ended in failure. Speaking to a reporter afterwards, Loulou said:

'Four occasions we tried the Eiger, four occasions we needed to retreat. However, I'm nonetheless alive!'

In 1965, Loulou joined a group of climbers from Geneve on a trip to the Caucasus Mountains in the Soviet Union. Having had left-wing political leanings all her life, it was said that she was as interested in experiencing life within Soviet society as in the climbing.

In 1977, aged 69, Loulou went on a two-month long expedition to the Sahara where she climbed a number of new routes in the Aïr Mountains of Niger including the first ascent of an impressive vertical tower rising straight out of the desert. This extraordinary climb was named the *'Tour Loulou'* in her honour.

She retired from her lifelong work at the International Labour Organisation in Geneva at the age of 62. After that she spent her days skiing whenever she could and climbing at Mont Salève. She continued to fight against injustices in society: during her seventies, she was still joining protests for a more just and equal world.

During a rare interview, Loulou was asked about her mountaineering life and the fact that there was so little record of her incredible career. To this, she replied:

'I climbed for climbing...I have no photographs...I think [having photographs] is all vanity – all is vanity.'

Unfortunately a serious skiing accident finally put an end to Loulou's outdoor activities. At which point she also stopped using her Alfa Romeo car which she was particularly fond of driving at speed!

Loulou Boulaz passed away in Geneva in 1991 at the age of 83. It had been an action packed life where she had accomplished so much in the world of both mountaineering and skiing. Her ascent of so many extremely challenging routes has given her the title of *'Queen of the North Faces.'* Loulou was undoubtedly, one of the greatest alpinists of the twentieth century.

Aiguille Verte and Petit Dru, French Alps

Grandes Jorasses, French Alps

Loulou Boulaz

Loulou Boulaz and Raymond Lambert just before climbing the Grande Jorasses

North faces of Tre Cime di Lavaredo, Italian Alps

Loulou Boulaz, Chamonix Alps

Mont Salève, Geneva

Zinalrothorn in the Swiss Alps (Credit: Zermatt Museum)

Tour Loulou, Montagnes de l'Aïr, Niger

Chapter 26

Dot Butler

Dot Butler

It was like fitting a hand into a glove. Bushwalking and I were made for each other.

Dot Butler was an Australian bushwalker, mountaineer and conservationist during the last century. She gained a reputation for walking long distances barefoot in the Australian bush.

Early years

Dot was born in Sydney in 1911, one of five children who all enjoyed a constant stream of childhood outdoor adventures. With no gender distinctions, both girls and boys carried out a series of fearless exploits climbing obstacles such as chimneys, telegraph poles, trees and even giant industrial cranes – all barefoot. When not at school Dot and her siblings enjoyed freedom from dawn to dusk, exploring their immediate environment and having outdoor escapades.

She found success at school, being particularly gifted at sport, and went on to study clerical skills in college. In her spare time she became part of the Bondi Beach Acrobatic Team and a winter swimming club called the Bondi Icebergs.

Dot began her working life in an office and earned enough money for her first great adventure. For two weeks she cycled barefoot around Tasmania on her own. She lived frugally and camped in out-of-the-way locations. Considering it was the 1930s, this was an audacious undertaking.

Wanting to stretch her wings further, for her twenty-first birthday Dot cycled alone to Mount Kosciuszko, Australia's highest mountain. The journey was just short of 500 kilometres, and it took her three and a half days. Arriving during the ski-season, Dot decided to try her hand at downhill skiing. Although it felt strange having wooden skis attached to her feet, after three days she was persuaded by other young people she had met to take part in a ski race. Being unsure, she asked the official starter,

'What do I have to do?'

'Just stand upright and keep going until you get through the tape,' came the reply.

Completing her downhill dash but not knowing how to stop, she carried on skiing until eventually coming to a halt on the flat.

To her great surprise, Dot was informed that she had actually won the Women's Downhill Championship!

Bushwalking

In 1931 Dot joined the Sydney Bush Walkers Club. During the Great Depression bushwalking was becoming a popular pastime at a time when some Australians were seeking a form of low-cost recreation. Dot once admitted, *'It was like fitting a hand into a glove. Bushwalking and I were made for each other.'*

Usually during weekends, bushwalkers walked long distances in challenging countryside then camped overnight. Continuing her childhood habit, Dot preferred to go barefoot and became known as the *'Barefoot Bushwalker'*. Eventually, she became one of only two women in the legendary 'Tigers' bushwalkers in the Sydney Bush Walkers Club. This select group was famed for covering extraordinarily long distances over rugged terrain and at great speed. Many outings took place in the Blue Mountains where the Tigers were filling in the gaps of unmapped areas. Some of the treks were up to 120 kilometres long and required gaining thousands of metres of elevation in tough, untracked and uncharted terrain.

In 1936, a few of the bushwalkers travelled to the Warrumbungle Range north-west of Sydney for some rock-climbing. The main aim of the trip was to ascend the yet-unclimbed Crater Bluff, a sheer volcanic rock fortress 955 metres in height and Dot was invited because of her natural climbing ability. She and a fellow bushwalker worked out a suitable route up the massive block of rock by following cracks, obvious holds, ledges and chimneys – and of course she climbed barefoot.

For Dot it was a new experience being roped to a climbing partner.

Inch by inch we edged along, clinging to scarcely perceptible ledges...feeling our way in those places we couldn't see for fear of upsetting our balance...

Eventually, they reached the top, built a cairn and lit a fire to inform those below of their success. Dot once expressed her philosophy regarding footwear whilst rock-climbing:

Rocks are my friends...They tell me what I can and can't do. People who climb in boots...are cutting themselves off from that contact.

Dot always encouraged others to bush walk. On one occasion in 1938, she walked 64 kilometres around a park in Sydney in ten hours. After that, she slept in the open in a forest before completing a taxing bush walk the following day. Her weekend of action was covered by the newspapers with the aim of encouraging more women to take up bushwalking.

Southern Alps of New Zealand

During the Christmas period of 1937, wanting to scale greater heights, a group of the bushwalkers travelled to New Zealand. After trekking and climbing some of the lower peaks on the South Island, they moved to the Southern Alps. This was an entirely new experience in higher mountains where they had to negotiate glaciers, crevasses and snow and ice features. It was also a place where Dot had to wear boots! After making their way up the Tasman Glacier, the party successfully climbed Hochstetter Dome at 3834 metres in height.

During this period of her life, Dot successfully trained as a physiotherapist and founded the Sydney Bush Walkers Magazine. Remembering those New Zealand mountains, in 1939 Dot moved there and took on clerical and physiotherapy work before being offered a job as a mountain guide in the Southern Alps.

As a guide, Dot accompanied tourists to various areas in the mountains and carried supplies up to mountain huts. When not at work she ascended peaks with different partners, including Mount Barff (2252 metres), Mount Aspiring (3033 metres) and

Malte Brun (3199 metres), and made mountaineering history by becoming the first woman to climb the West Peak of Earnslaw (2819 metres).

Wanting relief from wearing climbing boots, she made a barefoot solo climb of Mount Troas at 2243 metres, and climbed Aoraki/Mount Cook at 3724 metres, the highest of all New Zealand's mountains. Dot described the view from its summit:

...the sea stretching very blue and soft to the far horizon, while to north and south and east lay range after range of snowy peaks and glaciers and misty valleys.

Later in her life, a 1733 metre high mountain in the South Island, Mount Dot, was named after her.

Back to Australia

In 1941 Dot returned to Australia where she continued bushwalking whenever she could. As well as finding further work as a physiotherapist, she completed a course at Sydney University. There she met lecturer, economist and fellow bushwalker Ira Butler, but their relationship was interrupted when Ira, who was working for the war effort, was posted to Melbourne.

After he proposed by letter, Dot decided to ride her bike almost 900 kilometres from Sydney to Melbourne in order to marry him. She found employment as a physiotherapist in the city; later, when she was six months pregnant, she returned to Sydney, completing 350 kilometres of the trip by bicycle. Dot once calculated that during the Second World War, she cycled around 32,000 kilometres!

The couple had four children, during which time Dot was absorbed in raising her family, but wherever possible she introduced them to the delights and excitement of the great outdoors. The children grew up to be as self-reliant, adventurous and passionate about the natural world as their mother.

By the mid-1950s, Dot once again had the time to enjoy bushwalking. During this period, she remembered the words she had once heard a New Zealand guide jokingly make about her compatriots: *'The Franz Josef Glacier...contains 3672 crevasses and there is an Australian down every one!'*

After such an obvious affront, Dot decided to improve the mountaineering skills of her fellow Australians. She started by persuading the New Zealand Alpine Club, of which she was a member, to open an Australian section; the aim was to teach alpine skills and train members before their visits, enabling budding Australian climbers to cope better in the Southern Alps.

In 1956, Dot led the first of these newly trained parties on a seven-week trip to the New Zealand mountains. She continued this training for most of the following 25 years, often accompanying them on their annual Christmas trips.

Another facet of Dot's outdoor life was her becoming a member of the Bushwalkers Search and Rescue, and she was often called upon if a rescue required rock climbing. The most spectacular of these took place in 1962, in the Kananga Gorge around 180 kilometres from Sydney, after a young man fell off a cliff. He was successfully rescued after a complicated stretcher manoeuvre carried him out of the gorge.

Dot was also involved in setting up the Volunteer Bushfire Brigade.

Adventures further afield

As an economist, Dot's husband, Ira, often had to travel worldwide. Dot sometimes accompanied him, taking the opportunity to seek out foreign adventures. One such trip was to France; while her husband attended a conference, Dot went to the French Alps where she met up with a New Zealand friend. The pair traversed the Aiguille de Grépon at 3482 metres in height;

fortunately this classic route was mainly on rock because Dot had no crampons!

After attending a crash course in Spanish in Sydney, Dot organised an Australian mountaineering expedition of nine climbers to the South American Andes. The 1969 trip was a resounding success: 27 ascents were made on different mountains of Peru's Cordillera Vicabamba. Thirteen of these climbs were first ascents and were mostly over 5500 metres in height.

After the expedition Dot continued on a journey around the world, which included solo cycling trips in both Ireland and Spain, before returning to Australia. Using the same 'around-the-world' ticket, she trekked in the Himalayas and cycled in Cambodia just before the Vietnamese war broke out in the region.

In 1970, a strong earthquake hit the Peruvian Andes where they had held their Australian expedition. In response to the tragedy, Dot set up a relief fund to assist in the recovery operation; it was still providing funds twenty years later.

In 1972, she visited Europe again and climbed the Fisteraarhorn, the South Peak of the Eiger, the Monk and the Jungfrau in the Swiss Alps in just four days. Moving on to Norway, Dot and friends climbed a number of mountains ranging from 1800–2400 metres in height.

During the summer of 1975, Dot, her daughter Rona and others canoed the Yukon River from Whitehorse to Dawson City in Canada, a month-long trip of 640 kilometres. She also spent time trekking in California's High Sierra. Whenever an opportunity arose, Dot was ready for adventure!

Conservation work, tragedies and her later life

All of her life, Dot maintained a deep affinity with the natural world and she campaigned tirelessly to protect the Australian environment, considering it incredibly important to protect the native flora and fauna within their natural landscapes. She said,

> *'I think the future for Australians will be in regeneration. We have to repair the damage we've done to the country.'*

During the 1930s, she had helped establish the Rangers' League, whose aim was to develop a greater awareness of caring for Australia's wild plants, mammals and birds. In Tasmania, she campaigned against the flooding of Lake Pedder and the consequences it would have on natural habitats. Dot also worked with others towards the establishment of Myall Lakes, Blue Mountains, Warrumbungles and other Australian national parks. In the 1980s, she helped protect tropical rainforest at Cape Tribulation in northern Queensland which eventually became a World Heritage Site. In the Kangaroo Valley in New South Wales, there is a *'Dot Butler Conservation Reserve'* named in her honour.

Unfortunately, Dot experienced a number of family deaths: her daughter Wendy drowned in a river accident in 1966; her husband Ira passed away in 1972; a year later, her son Norman suffered a lethal snake bite, and her other son, Wade, went missing whilst on a solo expedition to Tasmania. Continuing with her adventures helped Dot cope with her personal tragedies.

She often took part in urban climbing challenges with the Night Climbers of Sydney. This secretive group met after dark to scale city buildings and venture into underground sewers. In 1991, Dot celebrated her 80th birthday with them first by climbing the Sydney Harbour Bridge and then abseiling down it!

In 2008, at the age of 96, Dot died in Tasmania. It was the end of an action-packed life in the great outdoors. She had not only embraced bushwalking, mountaineering and conservation to the full but had also played a central role in developing these activities for her fellow Australians.

Dot's zest for life lived up to her chosen motto: *Energy begets energy.*

Acrobatic display on Bondi Beach, Dot is the fifth from the right (Credit: Colin Wood – Greenaissance)

Aoraki (Mount Cook) from Hooker Glacier Lake

Barefoot climbing Dot with partner with footwear

Dot Butler climbing barefoot (Credit: the Crag)

Dot writing her climbing log in the Andes, South America

Dot with fellow bushwalker holding a highly venomous snake

Dot, far left, with fellow guide Duncan Darroch escorting a group of women in the New Zealand Alps

*Mountaineering in Tasmania
(Credit: Colin Wood Greenaissance)*

Mountaineering in Tasmania, Mount Ossa

The 'Tigers' 1937. Dot is third from the right.

Chapter 27

Junko Tabei

Junko Tabei

Again and again I had to rest...Every step was agony, but I persuaded myself to continue...Then I took my last step to the summit of Mount Everest.

Junko Tabei was the first woman to climb Mount Everest. She was also the first woman to complete the 'Seven Summits', climbing to the highest point on every continent.

Early life

Junko was born in 1939 in Miharu, a small agricultural town in Fukushima in central Japan. She was one of seven children born into a family who ran a printing company. As a child, she was small in stature and suffered from a variety of illnesses, which included contracting pneumonia on several occasions.

Junko always enjoyed playing in the countryside surrounding her home. At school she wasn't particularly good at physical education but she became an accomplished musician; she was gifted at singing and learned to play the *koto,* a traditional Japanese stringed instrument.

At the age of ten, Junko joined a school visit to Mount Nasu, which had a profound impact on her life and started her lifelong passion for the mountains. Writing about the trip some years later, she commented:

When we reached the summit that day, I felt a joy of achievement that I had never experienced before.

Unfortunately, her adolescence and early adulthood weren't entirely happy. She gained a place at Showa Women's University in Tokyo where she studied English, as well as American literature, but she struggled to adjust to her new learning environment and to life in a big city. Having received medical advice, she left university and returned temporarily to her family home where she spent her days hiking in nearby forests and hills. This appeared to help settle her mind.

On her return to university Junko felt more invigorated and continued with her studies. Wanting to maintain her new hiking regime, she began taking Sundays off to walk in the countryside outside the city:

...my body quivered with the cool air of nature and the scent of the earth. I felt instantly alive as I found my pace and relaxed into each forward stride.

Climbing apprenticeship

In 1962, Junko joined a local climbing club. Her aim was to progress from the lower and easier 'green' mountains onto the more challenging 'white' mountains of Japan. As was usual at the time, the club was mainly made up of men and Junko encountered a lot of sexism. Some men refused to climb with her, others said it was no place for a woman, and there were some who assumed that any new female climber was only joining to find a husband.

Such attitudes didn't deter Junko; she simply wanted to gain enough climbing experience to ascend to ever-greater heights. She learned how to use an array of mountaineering equipment and completed a number of rock climbing routes in the Tokyo area, then more demanding outings before her club left for an ascent of Mount Fuji. She was taught how to climb on snow and ice and how to use winter equipment whilst staying safe.

Junko had realised her dream of climbing those white mountains! What she lacked in strength compared to her male counterparts she made up for in stamina and technique; she appeared to have a natural climbing ability.

There followed a whole raft of different climbs in a number of upland regions of Japan. Eventually Junko joined another climbing club, which had a much smaller group of very talented mountaineers. It was with this elite group that she started climbing to a whole new level. On one of her first trips she noted:

...an experience of firsts for me: new mountain, new partner, the use of etriers, and lead climbing on a difficult route.

Junko's mountaineering ability continued to evolve quickly. After a time, she began to climb with another female climber, Rumie Sasou, and together they completed a number of outstanding ascents, including new routes by an all-female team. Many days were spent on some of the most challenging climbing routes in Japan.

It was around this time she met Masanobu Tabei, a man who had made a name for himself as a gifted mountaineer. After a period of time they married; once again, Junko was defying societal convention because husbands were often selected by a girl's parents.

Junko and Masanobu agreed from the outset that marriage wouldn't curtail their mountaineering ambitions. Not long after their wedding, Masanobu travelled to Switzerland to climb the North Face of the Matterhorn but unfortunately he lost four toes after suffering frostbite. This accident, together with the tragic death of some of Junko's friends whilst climbing, didn't in any way diminish her passion for mountaineering. Indeed, she continued to climb with increased vigour.

Annapurna III

Having made her mark on the Japanese climbing scene, Junko was invited to join an all-female expedition to climb the 7,555 metre Annapurna III in the Himalayas. This proposed expedition was at an entirely different mountaineering level; it was a huge logistical undertaking with 138 people including eight female climbers, a doctor, a reporter, sherpas and porters. Each climber had to raise funds to cover the cost of the expedition.

Once beneath Annapurna III, the expedition members slowly established ever higher camps as they made their way up this Himalayan giant. Most of the team members had difficulty in acclimatising and found it necessary to descend in order to rest. When all the camps were finally established, the expedition leader, Eiko Miyazaki, selected Junko and fellow climber Hiroko Hirakawa, together with Sherpas Girmi and Pasang, for the assault team. The final push for the summit was extremely challenging with difficult rocks and boulders to negotiate and exceptionally hard ice but eventually they stood on the summit of Annapurna III. Triumph! They were the first women to ascend Annapurna III and the first Japanese party.

During the expedition's journey home, a note was handed to Junko from her husband, Masanobu. It congratulated her and concluded, *'Aim for an 8000er next'.* Her husband's encouragement helped to establish her next mountaineering dream.

<u>Mount Everest</u>

After meeting with others, it was decided to submit an application to the Nepali government to climb Mount Everest as the Japanese Women's Everest Expedition. The team would again be led by Eiko, with Junko as lead climber. Female mountaineers were selected from across Japan to put together the strongest possible team.

The expedition was eventually given permission to climb during the 1975 season. Around this time, Junko became pregnant and her life became exceptionally hectic: a suitable climbing team had to be assembled; an array of necessary expedition items for Everest needed to be found; Junko had to continue with her climbing and fitness preparation – and she needed to prepare and give birth to her baby girl, Noriko. Quite a list!

Part of Junko's training regime immediately before departing for Everest included running a 19-kilometre route three times per week with her husband and daughter following by car.

The Japanese Women's Everest Expedition team consisted of 14 climbers and one doctor. The expedition was desperately short of serious sponsorship; many corporations were unwilling to support it because traditional values questioned the whole idea of an all-woman expedition. Junko once summed up the common response: *Raise your children...rather than do something like this.*

Eventually a Japanese newspaper and a TV corporation agreed to support the expedition financially, which came as immense relief. The preparation was a challenge. Putting together expensive climbing equipment was a constant worry; Junko spent time making high-altitude gloves and other items rather than purchasing them. Finally, leaving Noriko in the capable arms of her husband, it was time to depart for Nepal. After so many months of frenzied preparation, the Japanese Women's Everest Expedition was on its way.

Junko and another member of the team travelled ahead to India to arrange transport for the vast amount of expedition equipment destined for Nepal. Eventually the entire team arrived in Katmandu and made their way to Everest Base Camp. From its position on the Khumbu Glacier, they started a steady climb to establish different camps up the peak following the South East Ridge Route.

The first challenge was through the unstable and potentially lethal seracs of the Khumbu Icefall, but they pressed on and established Camps II, III and IV further up the Khumbu Glacier. From Camp IV, in worsening weather, Junko retreated to Camp II in order to rest after the exertions of the ascent.

Whilst they slept at Camp II, they were abruptly woken by a loud noise. Avalanche! Snow and ice had shot down the mountainside, collapsing tents and bringing devastation to the entire camp. The climbers were shouting to each other to check if everybody was still alive but luckily they all appeared to be okay. Junko appeared to have suffered the most: she had severe bruising and was unable to walk.

It was suggested that everybody at Camp ll, including Junko, should go lower down the mountain to recover. Junko resisted this idea, realising that there wouldn't be enough time to descend, rest and then climb back up before the monsoon closed in.

Remarkably, after three days Junko was walking again! The assault party was selected, which included Junko, Yuriko Watanabe and Sherpa Ang Tsering. They continued up the mountain to Camp V at the South Col but, due to the limited number of oxygen bottles, Yuriko withdrew from the final push to the summit.

Junko and Sherpa Ang set off the following day from the South Col. The route was very steep and desperately challenging in the thin air, and the climbers had to dig deep both physically and mentally.

When they were level with the nearby summit of Llotse, they cleared enough space to erect their small tent for Camp VI. The confined spot meant that going to the toilet required one climber to belay the other from within the tent!

The following day, in deep snow, they reached the South Summit of Everest then climbed the precarious knife-edge ridge to the challenging Hillary Step. Continuing in soft snow and hard ice, and taking a lot of rests, they carried on:

Again and again I had to rest...Every step was agony, but I persuaded myself to continue...Then I took my last step to the summit of Mount Everest...My crampons bit into the snow as I firmly stood beside Ang Tsering. He stretched out his big mitt and we shook hands.

On the 16th of May 1975, Junko Tabei became the first woman to climb Mount Everest!

After the success of the Japanese Women's Everest Expedition there was a whirlwind of attention. Honours were bestowed upon Junko and Ang by both the King of Nepal and the Prime Minister of India, and there was overwhelming interest in the expedition's achievements in what was International Women's Year.

When Junko arrived back in Japan she was met with a barrage of reporters and TV crews. Amidst the frenzied scene were her husband, Masanobu, and her daughter Noriko, whom she had not seen for six months. Over the following months the interest continued with yet more interviews with the press and a formal meeting with Japan's Emperor and Empress.

Junko Tabei's life had changed irreversibly. As a naturally modest and self-effacing person, such adoration didn't come easy; she often referred to herself as simply the 38th person to scale Mount Everest rather than the first woman!

Life continued for Junko and her family. There was always interest in her Everest story and her opinions on mountain topics were often sought. In 1978, the family had an additional member when their son, Shinya, was born. Junko continued to climb, such was her passion and commitment to the mountains. Having scaled the highest summit in the world, there were no limits to her ambitions.

In 1981 she climbed Kilimanjaro, the highest mountain in Africa, and in the same year ascended Shishapangma in China, again becoming the first woman to climb the mountain and summiting her second Himalayan peak at over 8000 metres. There followed more successful ascents in the Himalaya before she climbed the 6961 metre high Aconcagua in Argentina, the highest point in South America in 1987.

The following year she climbed Dinali, the highest in North America. In 1991, Junko climbed the 4892 metre Vinson Massif, the highest peak in Antarctica, and in 1992 she climbed Carstensz Pyramid in Indonesia, the highest point in Oceania, and also Mount Elbrus, the highest in Europe. In doing so, Junko Tabei became the first woman to climb the 'Seven Summits', the highest points on every one of the world's continents. Another phenomenal achievement!

Even after achieving this mountaineering milestone, Junko didn't slow down. She continued to climb around the globe, including climbing her third 8000 metre peak, the 8188 metre high Cho Oyu in China. She was increasingly concerned about the impact climbing and tourism was having on mountain environments and in 1999 visited Everest Base Camp to research the pollution caused by expeditions. She also served as the director of the Himalayan Adventure Trust of Japan, which was committed to protecting fragile high-alpine environments from climbers and hikers. Even so, Junko continued to climb!

The mountains she ascended may have been getting a little lower but her enthusiasm remained. As the years unfolded, she took to climbing to the highest points of each country she travelled to, including Mount Ararat in Turkey, Ojos del Salado in Chile, Galdhopiggen in Norway, Moldoveanu in Romania, Mafadi in South Africa, Khuiten Peak in Mongolia, and Pico Mogoton in Nicaragua!

In 2015, during one of her last interviews, she explained:

...I am challenging myself to climb all the highest peaks of all the countries in the world. I am now 76, and have scaled the highest peaks in 76 countries.

In 2011, Junko started organising hikes for people who had been affected by Japanese earthquakes, and the following year she started an annual programme for high-school students who were victims of earthquakes. The intention was for the students to ascend the 3776 metre high Mount Fuji, Japan's highest mountain. The 2016 climb included many who had been victims of the Fukushima nuclear disaster; on this occasion, having only just completed extensive treatment for cancer, Junko only managed to climb to 3010 metres before having to descend. It was the last mountain of her life and she died a few months later at the age of 77.

Junko Tabei has become an icon of the mountaineering world. As a female climber with an extraordinary passion for the mountains, she has been a climbing trailblazer especially for women. She had tremendous determination and lived her life according to her own motto: *Do not give up – keep on your quest.*

Junko is, quite simply, a mountaineering legend!

Junko Tabei

Annapurna III

Mount Everest

Junko Tabei on top of Everest (Credit: Mamnick of Sheffield)

Mount Fuji, Japan

Mount Nasu, Japan